Copyright © 2024 by Richard Sherman

All rights reserved. No part of this book may be reprinted, reproduced, or utilized in any form or by any electronic, mechanical, or other means, now known or hereafter invented, or any information storage or retrieval system, without the express written consent of the author.

First Edition, March 2024

For information about reprints, purchasing, or speaking engagements visit www.NeverHomeHeroes.com
or email rich.rsphoto@gmail.com

Design by Ashton & Partners, San Anselmo, CA

ISBN 979-8-9898085-0-2

Printed in the USA

This book is dedicated to Michele who took time to help a stranger many years ago and changed the course of our lives forever. Thank you.

MEUSE - ARGONNE

INTRODUCTION | A JOURNEY OF GRATITUDE

PROLOGUE

October 2007: After a couple of long flights, I tumbled into a cab in Vancouver with a clumsy suitcase and an overstuffed briefcase, and gave the driver the hotel name.

"Where are you coming from?" the older driver asked, peering at me through the rearview mirror.

"New York," I said, as I sorted my gear in the back seat. "But I don't think Americans are very popular up here in Canada right now," I chuckled, referring to the anti-war sentiments late in George W. Bush's presidency.

"I love Americans," the old guy replied quickly and raised his head to look at me again in the mirror. It was then I noticed his glacier blue eyes. I was curious why, so I asked him. He proceeded to recount his story as a Ukrainian soldier fighting with the Russians against the Nazis in World War II. He explained that Ukrainians were second-class citizens in the Russian Army. We chatted a bit about the ongoing Second Gulf War and my experiences in the First Gulf War. They paled in comparison to what I learned from his stories.

"We had to fight," he shrugged. "We are Ukrainians. We fought against the Nazis to survive, and we fought for the Russians so they would not kill us," he said, once again looking in the rearview mirror with those piercing blue eyes.

He continued, "But we could never figure out the Americans. They came thousands of miles to fight in a war when they didn't have to." He shrugged his shoulders again and gestured, belying the confusion that still remained.

As we arrived at the hotel, he said, "The Americans...they had food...every day. We couldn't believe it. Here we were fighting on our own land, and we would go three, four days without any food from the Russians. But the Americans had food every day. And, what they had, they shared with us."

We pulled to a stop and he said again, "No, I love the Americans." I thanked him for sharing his remarkable story and dragged my gear out of the back seat. When I looked up, he was standing outside the cab with his hand extended, "I want to say thank you to America."

This experience swims in my head, resurfacing into consciousness several times a year. Over the years, I have recounted this story dozens of times to family, friends, and strangers alike. It is never far from my mind.

Fast forward a decade, and a thought—a paradox, more accurately—popped into my head. *How do you thank someone whom you have never met?* Now when people ask where this project began, I tell them it was from my experience in Vancouver and from this question that kept bouncing around in my head. Over more than five years, I made eight trips to three continents to visit all 23 American overseas military cemeteries. This project is a journey of personal gratitude. I also hope it is a reminder to everyone of the profound sacrifices made by these heroes for our freedom and for the freedom of countless people in distant lands.

I fear that the world wars are drifting into history for young people in America—the overwhelming majority have never been enriched by a conversation with a great-uncle or -aunt, a grandfather or grandmother who served in World War II. For without direct interaction, these events, these sacrifices, these achievements become nebulous, abstract, disorganized, ambiguous, incomprehensible. It is often said, "We must never forget," but how can someone "not forget" if they have never been taught in the first place? Thus, on this journey of gratitude, I have also realized that *Never Home: Remembering the Military Heroes Who Never Returned* is also a duty, an obligation to those who perished in war.

This project would not have been possible without the outstanding men and women of the American Battle Monuments Commission (ABMC) who are dedicated to honoring those who fell in battle overseas. They have been generous in supporting this work, are steeped in knowledge, and have been friendly and welcoming in every location.

In gratitude…
Richard Sherman
February 2024

PREFACE

There are 207,621 men and women memorialized in America's 23 overseas World War I and World War II cemeteries. Sadly, this includes 83,441 listed on the Walls of the Missing and roughly 7,500 interred as "Unknowns."

The US military upholds a tradition of remembering those who served before us. The accounts of valor in prior wars motivate today's service members to uphold their examples of courage, discipline, and sacrifice. I am a former Navy officer who served during the First Gulf War. I can honestly say that the individuals who have served or are serving our nation are never far from my mind. My father served in Korea, his brother in World War II, and my godfather in Vietnam. They spoke little of their experiences, but often mentioned their love for the United States Navy.

The impetus to undertake this project dates back to 2007 when I met a Ukrainian cab driver in Vancouver who fought in World War II. He told me how much he loved America and shared stories of the courage and generosity shown to him and his fellow soldiers by American troops. Several years later, I approached a milestone birthday and a thought entered my mind: How do you thank someone you have never met? This book then is my journey of gratitude. I made eight trips to three continents to visit our overseas military cemeteries that hold the remains of Americans who never made it home from the world wars. As a professional photographer, I took my camera gear with me so that everyone could share the experience.

Called away from their homes to fight in distant lands, these Americans are true heroes. Today, the world often defines heroes as people who are great at doing something we all wish we could do, like dunk a basketball, play in a band, or star in a movie. In contrast, these true heroes did a great job at something that no one would ever want to do. Today, the conversation and debate are about American rights, yet these distant cemeteries offer us a powerful reminder that citizenship also comes with great responsibilities.

There are countless history books that detail our nation's involvement in the world wars—I have dozens on my bookshelf. However, this is not a history book. For military families and friends who lose a loved one, the loss is never "history" to them. This book is structured as an emotional journey through the eight World War I and 14 World War II cemeteries.* My camera is the vehicle for this journey, and the layout is designed to evoke the emotions experienced on a visit to any of these cemeteries: from the moment you first glimpse the hallowed grounds, to your walk among the headstones, to the final moments when the magnitude of the loss hits you.

On the ensuing pages, we will remember our fallen heroes from the world wars primarily using imagery. I believe photography is the perfect language to capture the array of emotions one experiences when visiting these cemeteries. I have had conversations with many people who have visited Normandy

American Cemetery and they all seem to struggle for words when they attempt to describe their experiences. An image may be worth a thousand words, but it also captures complex emotions that lack specific descriptors.

The second chapter, "A Walk Among the Headstones," includes brief vignettes of several dozen individuals who have still never made it home. The fallen heroes featured in this book are chosen to be inclusive so we connect with them as individuals and not identify them solely as combatants. I contend they deserve more than to be remembered as a statistic in a history book or magazine article. They were brothers and sisters, sons and daughters, husbands and wives, aunts and uncles, and lovers. They had names. Let us remember them.

It has been my privilege to visit our fallen heroes in their final resting places. The experiences of visiting each one, of researching their stories, of chatting with my friends and family as well as the loved ones of the fallen heroes, have added immeasurably to my life.

So let us now begin this journey together, but let us also commit to each other that we will never forget the individuals who sacrificed everything.

Suresnes American Cemetery holds the remains of individuals from both world wars.

The term "American Cemetery" has been excluded on photography pages.

FOREWARD

There is a shop-worn quote about military service which goes something like this:

> "A veteran is someone who, at one point in their life, wrote a blank check made payable to the United States of America, for an amount up to and including their life."

Too many who fought in our wars had that check cashed, and many who perished were buried overseas, far from their homes.

According to the American Battle Monuments Commission (ABMC), there are approximately 124,000 American service members buried in the 23 American world war cemeteries located in eight foreign countries (since the Korean War, we no longer bury our brave dead overseas.). This book serves to educate us about the incredible sacrifices of so many during World War I and World War II. I have had the opportunity to visit a number of these overseas cemeteries and I always come away awed by the immense sacrifice of these service members, and just as importantly, by their families.

My own family has seen the impact of losing a close family member during an overseas war. My mother-in-law lost her brother, Oliver "Jack" Pitts, a US Marine, during the Battle of Cape Gloucester on New Britain Island in early 1944. She still remembers the impact his death had on her mother who was stricken with what doctors said was simply a broken heart. Jack was buried on that battle-strewn island. After the war, his mother worked hard to have Jack's body brought back home to be buried in the family plot at their church just down the road from their home. She knew that another burial would cause renewed sadness, but she wanted to have her son nearby, if possible. Years later, Jack's sister, my mother-in-law, named her only son, Dwight Oliver.

In my own family, my father served on the USS Evans (DD-552) in the Pacific theater. The Evans was destroyed by kamikazes during the Battle of Okinawa on May 11, 1945 after it and another ship were attacked by 150+ Japanese planes. Both ships and their crews fought valiantly and accounted for at least 42 kills before running out of ammunition. The Evans was hit by four kamikazes and put out of action, yet the crew saved the ship from sinking. Tragically, 32 crew members were killed and 27 were severely wounded.

I tell this story of the USS Evans, because four years later, my father, still in the Navy, was engaged to marry my mother. According to my grandmother, my father told his future wife to just pick a wedding date and he would be there. Later, when she told him that she had chosen May 11, 1949, he started to cry and begged her to pick another date because he could not be joyous on the anniversary of that tragic day off of Okinawa when he lost so many close shipmates.

Tens of thousands of American families have their own stories of lost loved ones. Many never had an opportunity to visit the grave of their service member interred in one of the overseas military cemeteries. That is why this book is so important, not just for these families, but for younger generations as well. Over 405,000 Americans lost their lives during World War II. Nearly 93,000 are interred in these overseas cemeteries. This does not include those WWII service members lost to an unofficial "cemetery," the ocean. It is estimated that over 75,000 sailors were either lost on ships sunk in action or were buried at sea by their shipmates. During my 36 years as a naval officer, I would ponder this loss as my ships plowed through the seas where war once raged.

I started with the trite saying about veterans having written blank checks. I much prefer to describe their sacrifices by quoting President Abraham Lincoln in one of the greatest (and shortest) speeches ever by an American political leader, "The Gettysburg Address." Lincoln said:

> *"It is rather for us to be here dedicated to the great task remaining before us–that from these honored dead we take increased devotion to that cause for which they gave the last full measure of devotion–that we here highly resolve that these dead shall not have died in vain."*

This wonderful book, *Never Home: Remembering the Military Heroes Who Never Returned* by Richard Sherman gives us and future generations the opportunity to embrace Lincoln's plea for remembrance of the great sacrifices of those who gave their "last full measure."

Vice Admiral Doug Crowder, US Navy (Ret.)

XIV

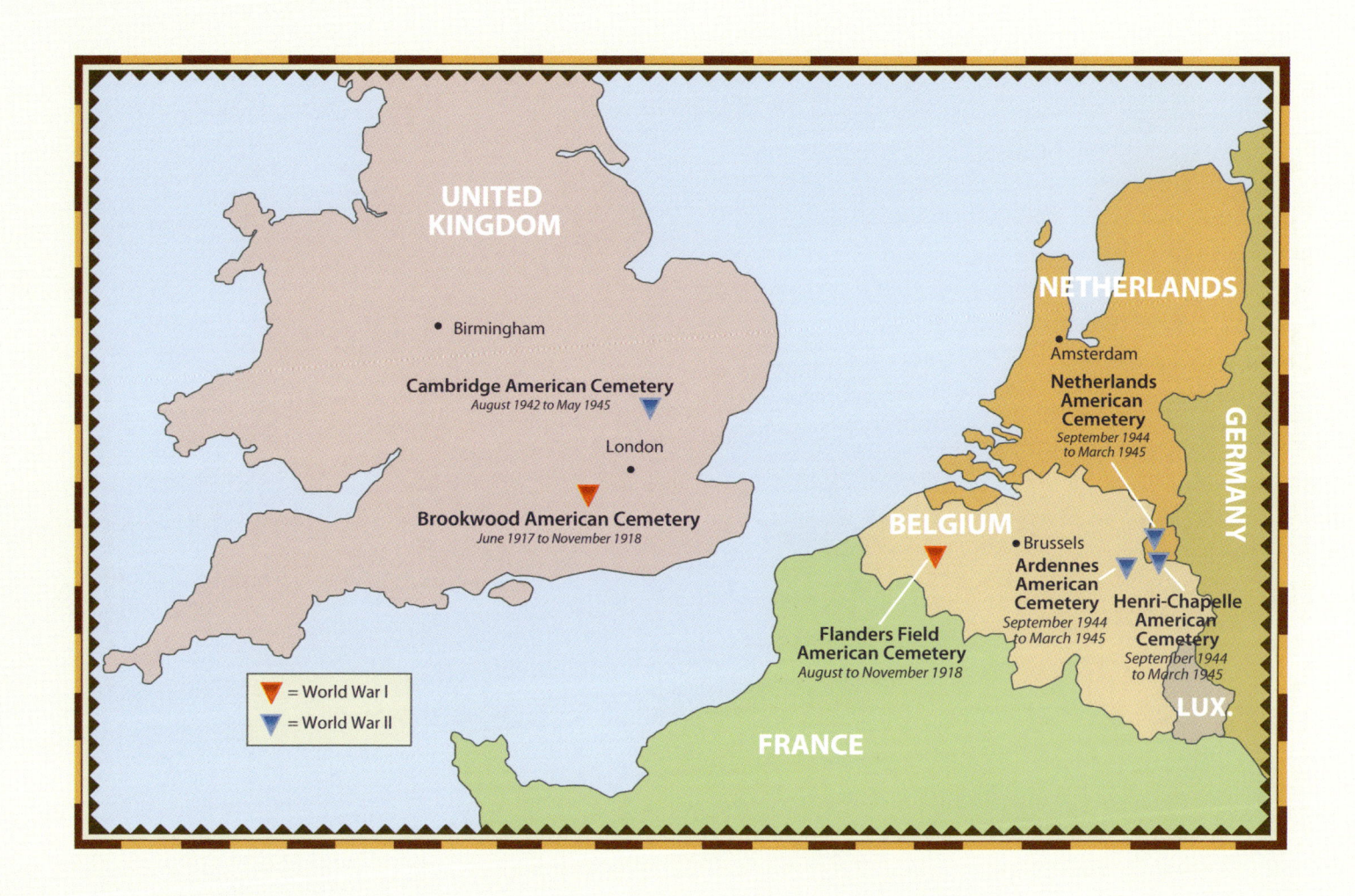

XV

Somme American Cemetery
May to October 1918

Luxembourg American Cemetery
December 1944 to March 1945

Normandy American Cemetery
June to August 1944

Oise-Aisne American Cemetery
August to September 1918

Meuse-Argonne American Cemetery
September to November 1918

Suresnes American Cemetery
Both WWI and WWII

St. Mihiel American Cemetery
August to September 1918

Lorraine American Cemetery
September 1944 to March 1945

Aisne-Marne American Cemetery
May to September 1918

Lafayette Escadrille Memorial
April 1916 to February 1918

Brittany American Cemetery
July to August 1944

Epinal American Cemetery
September 1944 to May 1945

BELGIUM
GERMANY
LUX.
FRANCE
SWITZERLAND
Paris

▼ = World War I
▼ = World War II
▼ = Both World Wars

XVI

XVII

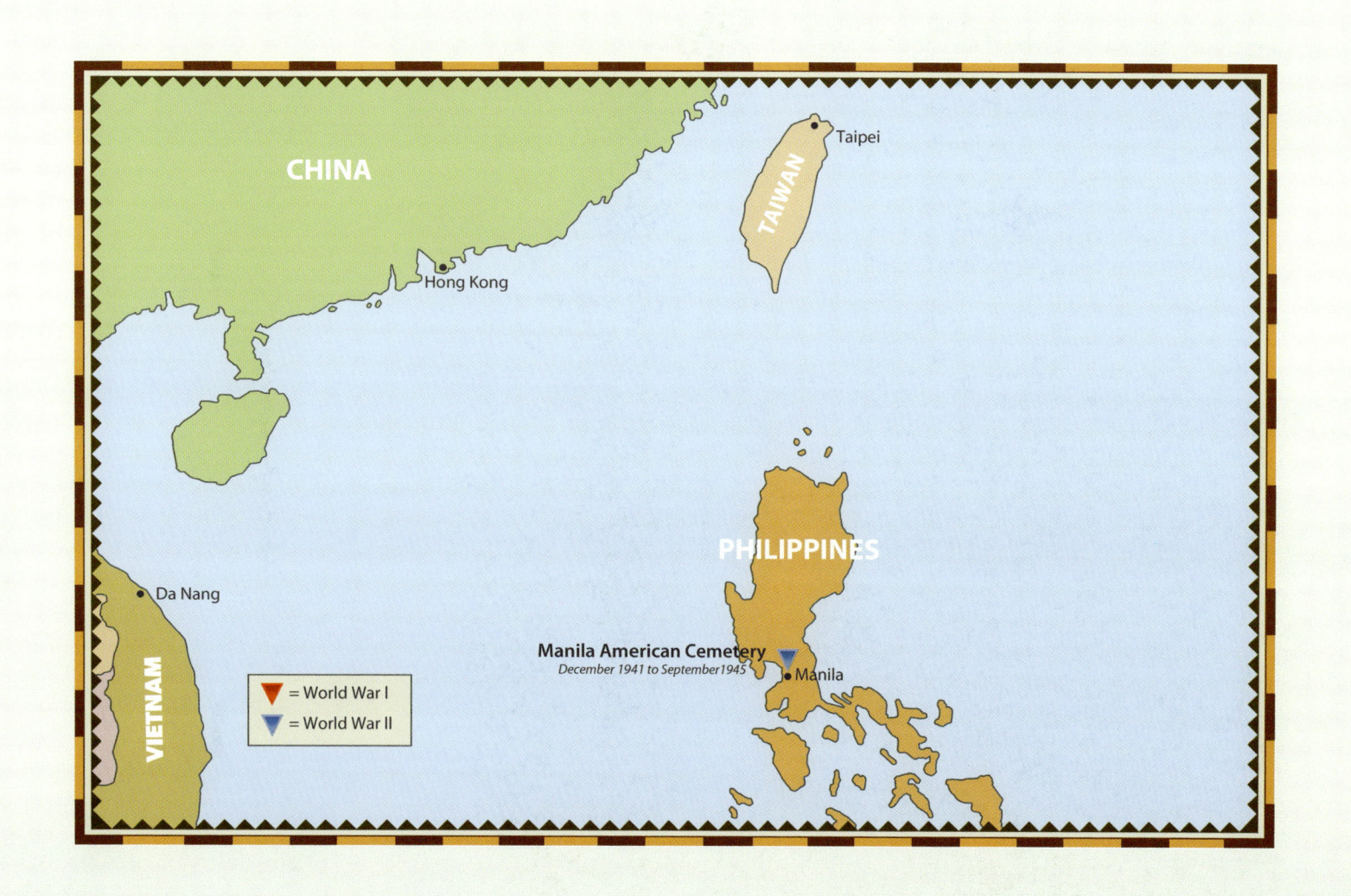

ST. MIHIEL

> Only the dead have seen the end of war.

PLATO

SOMME

CHAPTER ONE | IN THE COMPANY OF HEROES

"This war, like the next war, is a war to end war."

UK PRIME MINISTER DAVID LLOYD GEORGE, 1916

NORMANDY

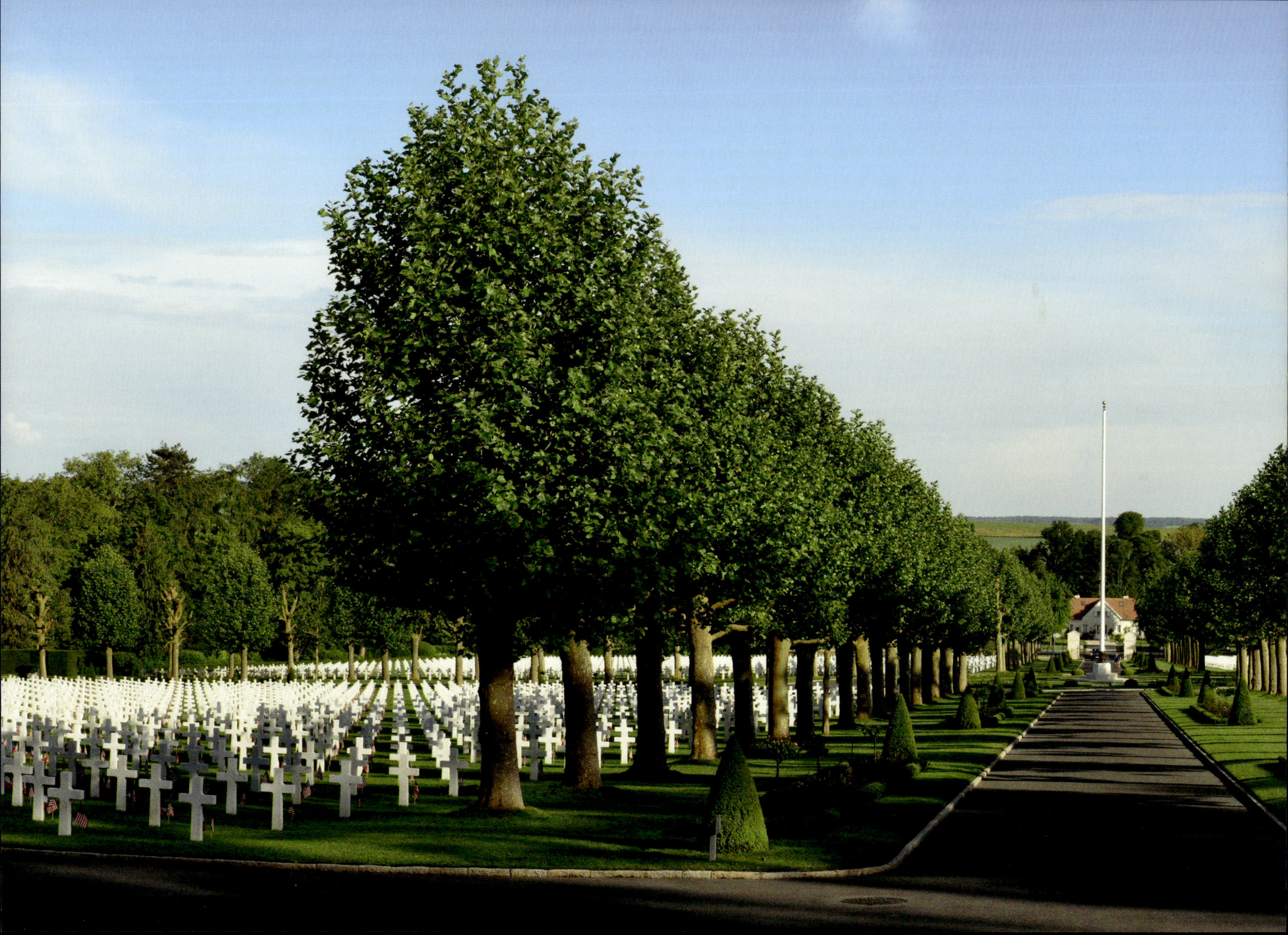

OISE - AISNE

ST. MIHIEL

ST. MIHIEL

ST. MIHIEL

AISNE - MARNE

AISNE - MARNE

LORRAINE

LAFAYETTE ESCADRILLE

A LA MEMOIRE
DES HEROS
DE L'ESCADRILLE LA FAYETTE
MORTS POUR LA DEFENSE
DU DROIT ET DE LA LIBERTE
MCMXIV
MCMXVIII

NETHERLANDS

FLORENCE

NORTH AFRICA

BROOKWOOD

SURESNES

21

FLANDERS FIELD

ARDENNES

CAMBRIDGE

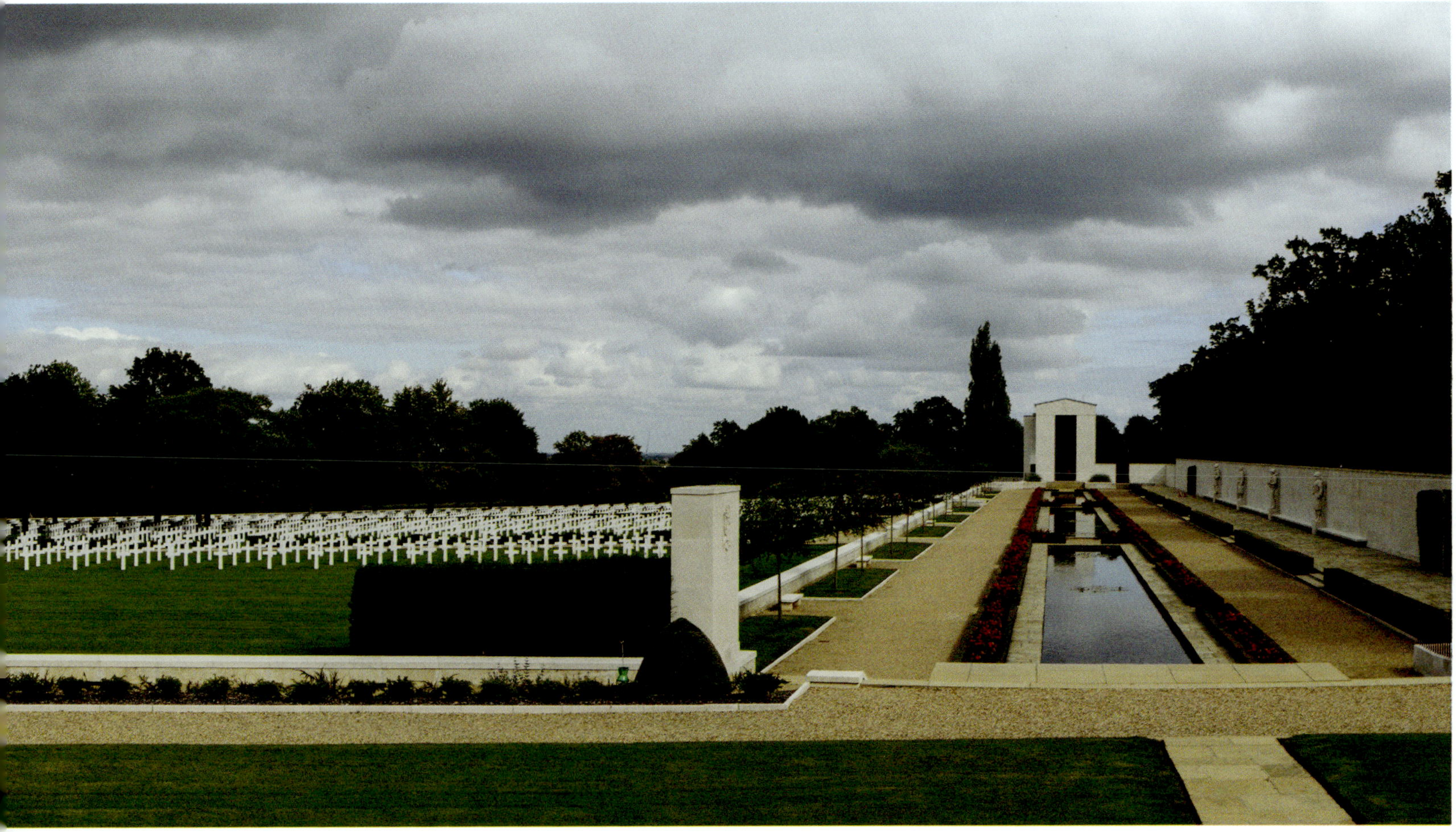

NETHERLANDS

MANILA

FLANDERS FIELD

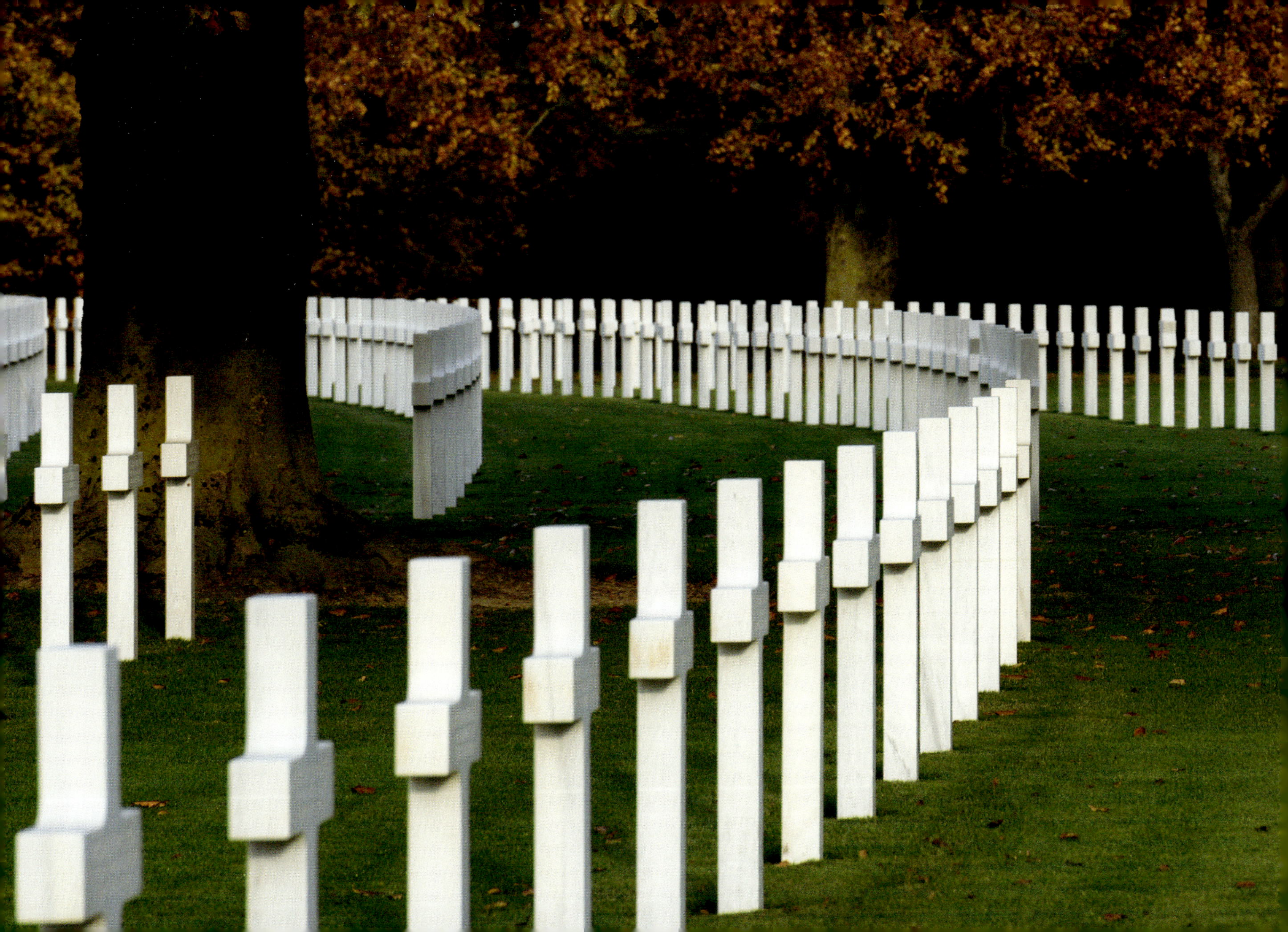

HENRI - CHAPELLE

NORMANDY

SOMME

BRITTANY

NORMANDY

ST. MIHIEL

NORMANDY

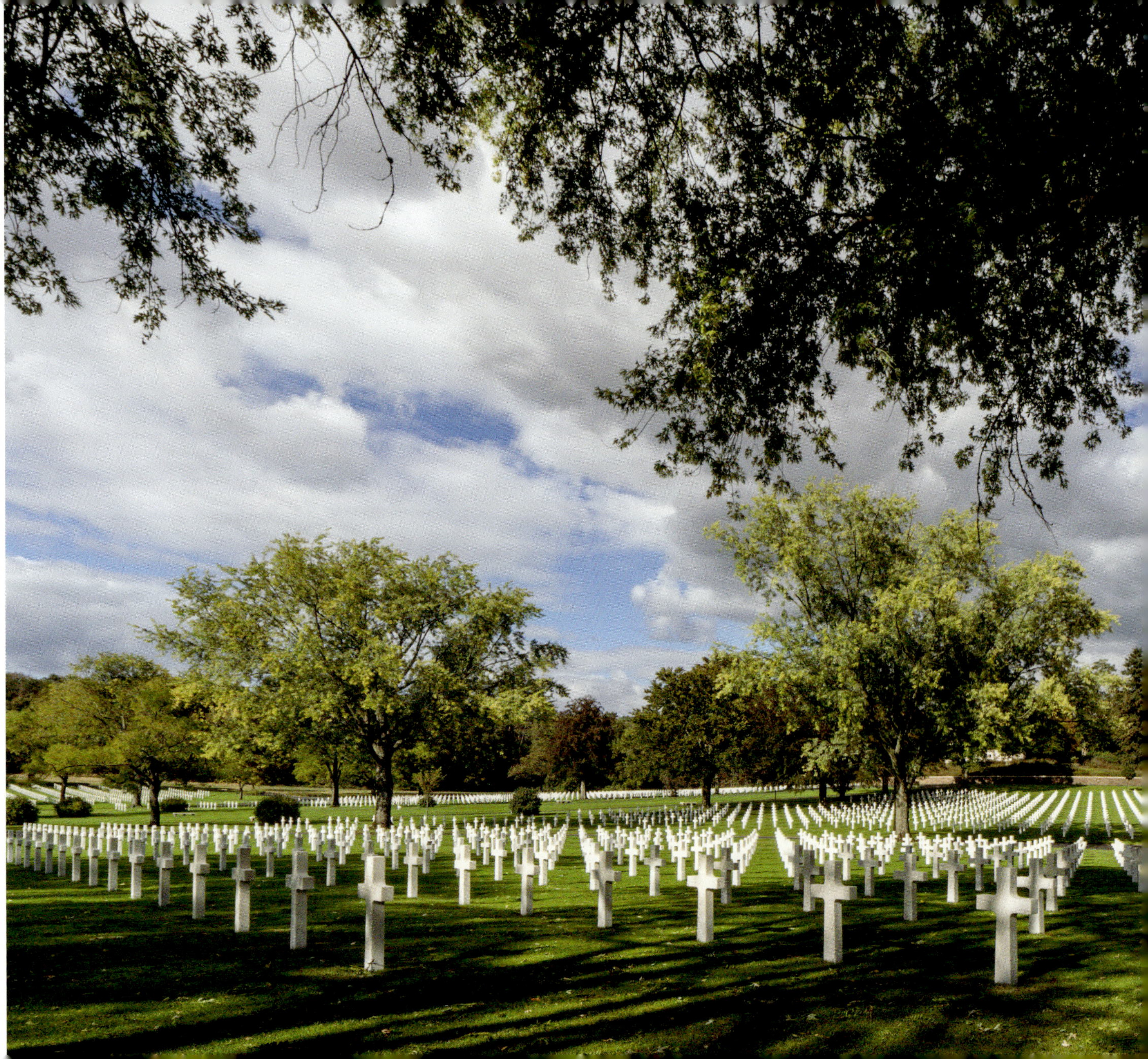

LORRAINE

ST. MIHIEL

SOMME

CAMBRIDGE

SICILY - ROME

SICILY - ROME

MANILA

NORMANDY

WORLD WAR II
VETERAN
WORLD WAR II
VETERAN
WORLD WAR II
VETERAN

OISE - AISNE

" Those who have long enjoyed such privileges as we enjoy forget in time that men have died to win them.

PRESIDENT FRANKLIN D. ROOSEVELT

HENRI - CHAPELLE

CHAPTER TWO | A WALK AMONG THE HEADSTONES

CHARLES L. SUMMERS
2 LT AIR CORPS
PENNSYLVANIA MAY 4 1942

FIRST AMERICAN KIA IN EUROPE DURING WWII

2LT Charles Summers, USAAF
May 4, 1942
Netherlands American Cemetery

Charles L. Summers was the first American to die in combat overseas during World War II. He served as an Observer on board the Royal Air Force's (RAF) Lockheed Hudson V AM530 reconnaissance planes.

Summers was born in Cedar Rapids, IA in 1918. He had a sister, Edna Mae, who was two years older. In the late 1920s, the family moved to California where their father managed a service station in Pasadena. Summers graduated from Pasadena Junior College in 1938, and then the University of California, Berkeley in 1940 with a degree in Electrical Engineering. He was a member of the American Institute of Electrical Engineers, the precursor to today's IEEE. In August 1941, he joined the Army Reserve's Signal Corps and was transferred to the Army Air Corps to become a radar specialist. He was sent to England in October 1941 to support the RAF. On May 4, 1942, he was on a five-man sortie searching for German U-boats off the coast of the Netherlands as part of RAF Squadron 53 when their plane was shot down. All five bodies washed ashore, with Summers' body recovered on June 27th at Egmond aan Zee (Netherlands).

Summers was due to return to the US just six days later (May 10th) to marry his fiancée, Betty Casler of New Jersey. Charles Summers was 24 years old.

BOMBER CREW MEMBER

TSGT Ward Sackal, USAAF
December 31, 1943
Rhone American Cemetery

Ward Sackal and Christine Gorder fell in love while he was in aviation training in Arizona. The two teenagers were together for a few months in early 1943, going to dances and movies and spending time with Christine's family. They shared many interests, and both enjoyed playing the violin. When the 578th Bomber Squadron was sent to Europe, Ward left without saying goodbye. It was just too hard for him. He was an engineer aboard a B-24 Liberator that was shot down on New Year's Eve 1943.

For a couple of years, Christine did not know what had happened to her handsome boyfriend. She finally wrote the War Department in 1945 only to learn that he had been killed when his plane was shot down in theatre. Christine went on with life, but she never forgot about Ward. When she opened a trunk of old memorabilia in 2009, she discovered a photo of Ward, his air wings, and some of their letters. She began to piece together Ward's story and eventually found a "Sackal" who just might be a family member. Christine made a phone call. The phone was answered by Ward's niece and a new relationship began. She soon learned that Ward was buried in Rhone American Cemetery in Provence, and, less than a year later, she was standing in front of his headstone. She visited his grave each year from 2010 to 2019 and placed a flower at his headstone each time. When the global pandemic hit, her trips were curtailed, so she had the cemetery staff place a rose in front of Ward's headstone each month. That tradition continues today.

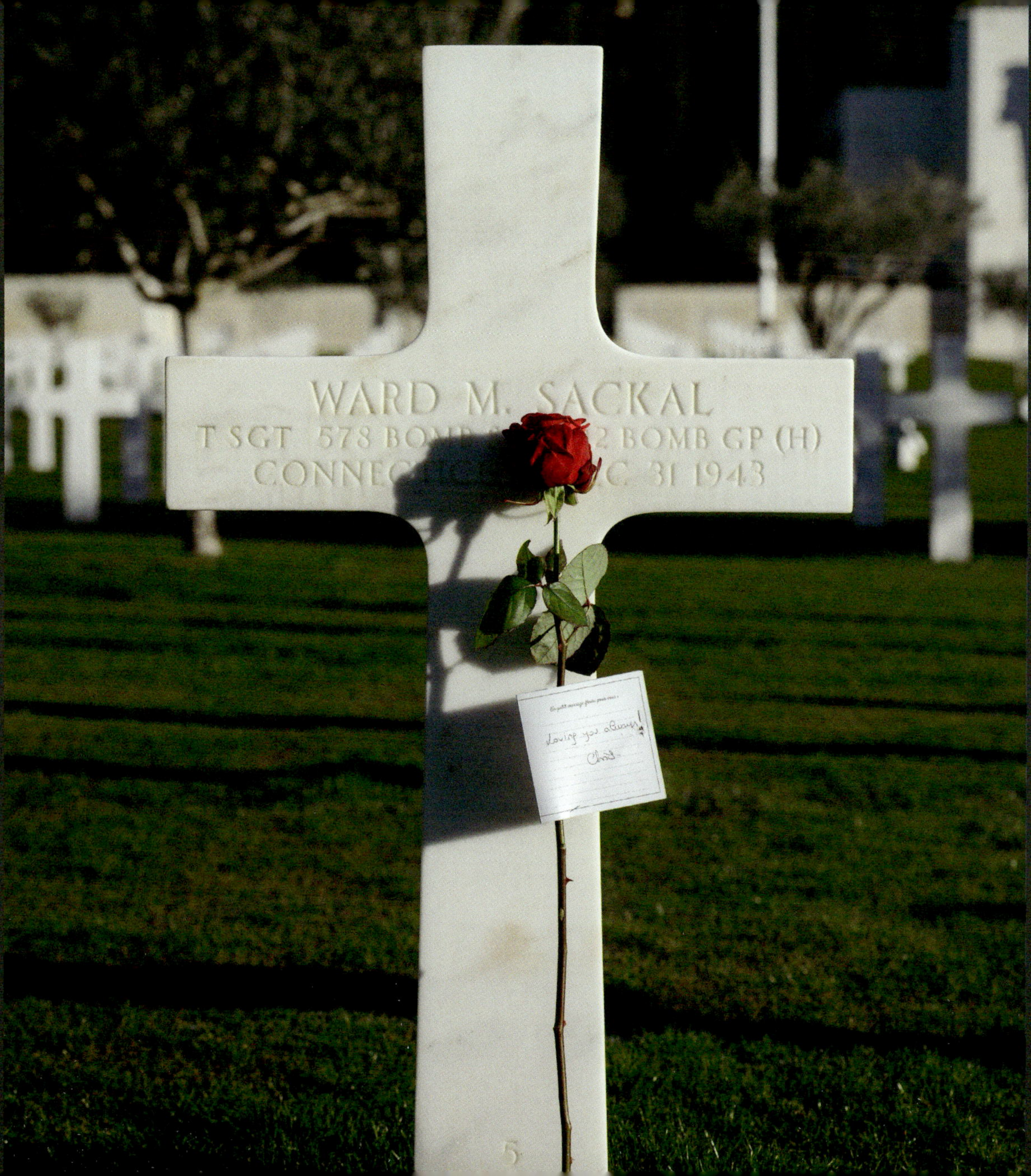
WARD M. SACKAL

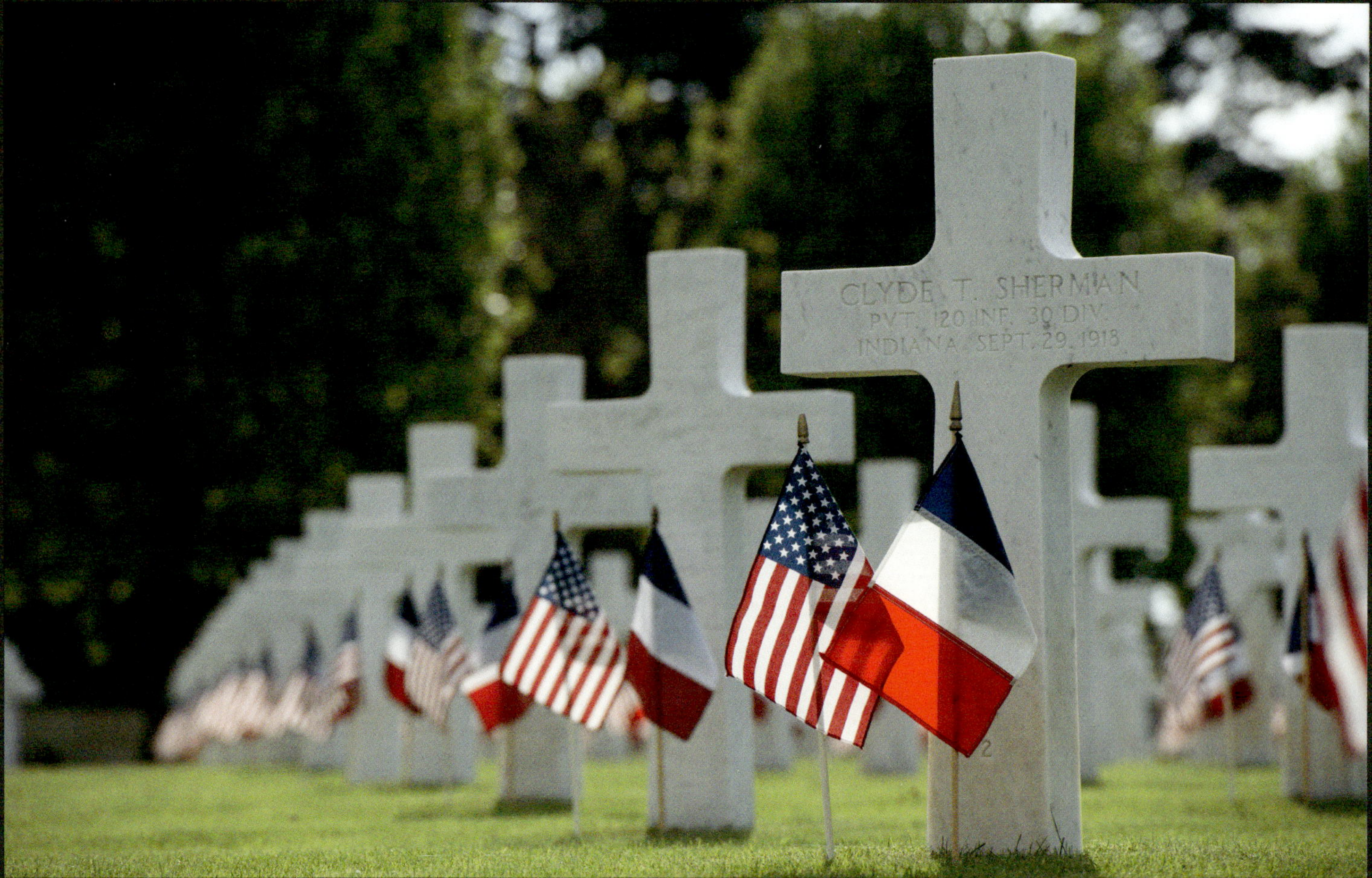
CLYDE T. SHERMAN
PVT. 120 INF. 30 DIV.
INDIANA SEPT. 29, 1918

WORLD WAR I INFANTRYMAN

PVT Clyde T. Sherman, USA
September 29, 1918
Somme American Cemetery

PVT Clyde Sherman was 26 years old when he was killed in action near Bellicourt (Belgium) as his unit, the 120th Infantry Regiment, attacked the famed Hindenburg Line on the Western Front. After two days of heavy allied bombardment of this renowned German defensive fortress, the 120th Infantry, accompanied by Australian troops, launched their offensive before dawn. After intense fighting, these units successfully broke this previously impenetrable, six-layer defense line, forcing the Germans to retreat and turning the tide of the war.

Before the war, Clyde Sherman was a steamboat clerk aboard *"Tell City"* and *"Tarascon"* (and perhaps other steamers) for the Louisville & Evansville Packet Company in New Albany, IN. He traveled the Ohio River frequently between Louisville and Cincinnati. Sherman's father, George, died in February 1918 while he was deployed. PVT Sherman was survived by a sister and three brothers, as well as his wife, Alma (née Borden), whom he married in June 1912. They had a daughter, Aletha, who was six years old when her father was killed.

AVIATION CHAPLAIN

CAPT Floyd Richert, USAAF
May 12, 1944
Cambridge American Cemetery

Floyd Richert was born on February 22, 1915 in Whitetail, MT. In 1941, he graduated from York College in Nebraska, where he was a member of the debate team and sang in the choir.

After college, Floyd briefly served the Church of the United Brethren in Christ located in Beach, ND, before joining the Army in 1942. As an Army Chaplain, he served first in North Africa and then in Sicily in 1943.

On May 12, 1944, he was a crew member of a Douglas C-47A Skytrain as part of the 316th Troop Carrier Group. During a paratroop training flight, his plane collided with another C-47 near their base at Cottesmore, England. All of the crew members on both aircraft were killed. Floyd was 29 years old.

FLOYD N. RICHERT
CHAPLAIN (CAPT) 316 TRP CARR GP
NORTH DAKOTA   MAY 12 1944

RAYMOND J. HANSEN
CHAPLAIN (CAPT) 8 INF 4 DIV
WISCONSIN JUNE 11 1944

CHAPLAIN

CAPT Raymond Hansen, USA
June 11, 1944
Normandy American Cemetery

Serving in the 4th Infantry Division, under the command of BGEN Teddy Roosevelt, Jr., Raymond Hansen was among the first waves of troops that landed near Utah Beach on D-Day. Although he survived the beaches of Normandy, he was killed in combat just five days later as his unit approached Eroudeville (France).

Before the war, Hansen was a minister of the Evangelical United Brethren Church in Augusta, WI. He spoke Danish, German, and English. He was loved by the troops and organized sports and other activities for them, which were known as "Padre's Hour." Raymond received the Purple Heart Medal and was survived by his wife, Leona. He was 31 years old.

CHAPLAIN

1LT Arthur Dieffenbacher, USA
July 5, 1944
Normandy American Cemetery

Arthur Dieffenbacher was a Protestant minister from Pennsylvania who joined the Army in July 1943. He grew up in Erie, PA and graduated from high school at the age of 15. He received a Master's Degree from Dallas Theological Seminary in 1932. He also worked as a missionary in China, where he met Junia White, whom he married in 1938. He returned to the US in the summer of 1940 after nearly eight years in China and lived in Wilmington, DE and Philadelphia, PA. His daughter, Sara Junia, was born in June 1941.

Dieffenbacher embraced Army training, including the dangerous "infiltration" course not required of chaplains. Remarkably, he earned the Army's Marksmanship Badge, a rarity among chaplains. From April to June 1944, Dieffenbacher served in England with the US Army and then went to France with the 330th Infantry Regiment, 83rd Division.

In a letter home, he wrote:

> "There are so many chances of getting hurt in war or in peace that which one affects you is by God's permission. Hence, I don't worry, but take all reasonable precautions and trust the rest to God. His will is best and His protection sufficient."

He was killed by artillery fire while attached to the 83rd Infantry in France. He was awarded the Purple Heart Medal and was survived by his mother, Mildred, his brother, Robert, his wife, and three-year-old daughter.

ARTHUR J. DIEFFENBACHER
CHAPLAIN (1 LT) 330 INF 83 DIV
PENNSYLVANIA JULY 5 1944

CIVILIAN DOCTOR

Dr. Crosby Church Whitman, Civilian
March 28, 1916
Suresnes American Cemetery

Crosby Church Whitman was born in Benicia, a small town northeast of San Francisco, in 1864. He spent his childhood in Virginia City and Carson City, NV. His father, Bernard Crosby Whitman, was a lawyer and then a judge on Nevada's Supreme Court.

Crosby attended prep school at Adams Academy in Quincy, MA, and then received his undergraduate degree in 1886 from Harvard University. The year before he graduated, his father passed away. After Harvard, Whitman moved to France and received his medical degree from the University of Paris in 1894. He enjoyed hunting and became a well-respected figure among the American community in Paris.

Crosby was the head of the American Hospital in Neuilly (near Paris) when the Great War started. The American Hospital was incorporated in 1913 to care for the large number of Americans living and studying in France. During the war, the 50-bed hospital treated wounded soldiers and officers, including many of the casualties from the Battle of the Marne. Dr. Whitman not only treated soldiers, he also paid for apparatus for some amputees with his own money and served on the staff of the Franco-Belge Dispensary that aided war refugees. He reportedly worked long days and nights to care for the soldiers. Finally convinced to take a break from his duties for a few days by his associates, Dr. Whitman died from heart failure in March 1916.

CROSBY CHURCH WHITMAN
DOCTOR Fr. RED CROSS HOSPITAL 79
FRANCE MARCH 28, 1916

IRVING I. SHURE
MAJ 94 GEN HOSP
N.C. JULY 27 1944

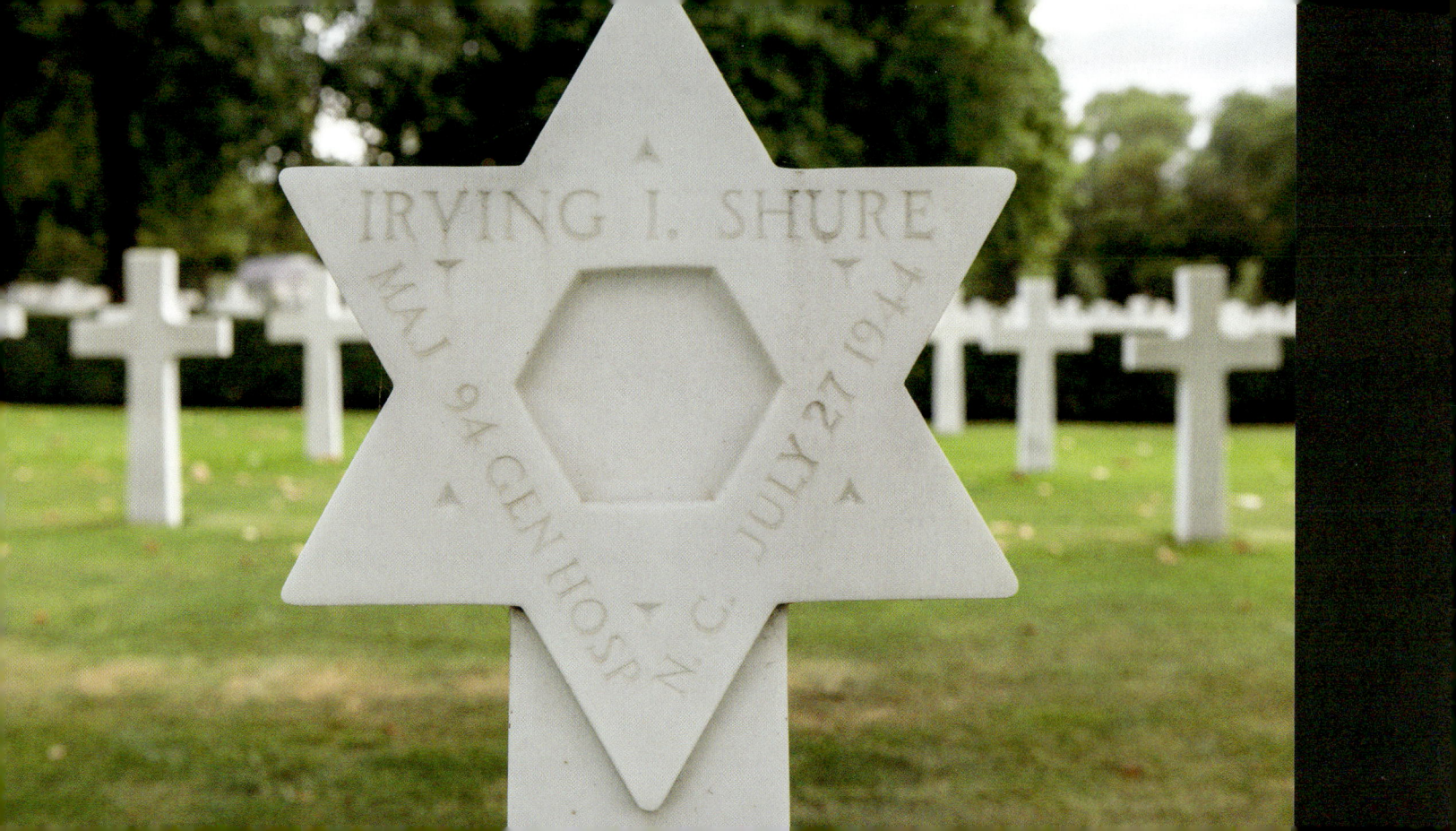

EENT DOCTOR

MAJ Irving Shure, USA
July 27, 1944
Cambridge American Cemetery

Irving Shure lived in the tiny community of Bethel, NC, and was commissioned an officer in the Reserve Officer Medical Corps in 1939. A native of Virginia, he graduated from Virginia Polytechnic Institute. Shure then received his medical degree from Medical College of Virginia in 1933 and did his internship at Trinity Hospital in Brooklyn, NY.

He lived in Bethel with his wife, Shirlevan. Dr. Shure had a horse and was a member of the town's bowling team, as well as the Rotary Club and Masonic Lodge.

His mother, Yetta, had moved to Bethel from Rocky Mount, NC in 1937 to be close to her son. Unfortunately, she passed away at the age of 55 in April 1940, not long before Irving reported for military duty in August 1941 at Camp Polk Station Hospital in Louisiana. He was appointed Chief of the Eye, Ear, Nose & Throat Section.

During the war, he was a Major with the US Army 94th General Hospital in Scotland. He was on board a C-47A Skytrain that was evacuating patients–mainly injured infantrymen—from France to Prestwick, Scotland, when the aircraft crashed near Portpatrick with the loss of all on board.

FLAG OFFICER

BGEN Edmund W. Searby, USA
September 14, 1944
Epinal American Cemetery

"From his example and indomitable spirit, [all front-line troops] derived additional inspiration and zeal to seek out, close with, and destroy the enemy."
Silver Star Citation for Edmund Searby

Born in Berkeley, CA, Edmund Searby graduated from the United States Military Academy at West Point in 1918, just as the US began combat operations in World War I. Searby loved horses and won many awards at horse shows while also enjoying polo. He was an excellent shooter and was often Master of the Hunt.

Searby was promoted to Brigadier General in February 1943 and was Division Artillery Commander for the 80th Infantry Division. After leading his men up a hill into direct artillery fire, he was killed in close combat during the Battle of Mousson Hill (near Nancy, France). BGEN Searby is one of the few flag officers interred in American cemeteries overseas. At the time of his death, he left behind a daughter and twin sons.

"...(H)e stands up like he was shootin' targets and [Searby] aims at the guy and a machine gun just literally cut him in half. He was dead before he dropped down beside me to the ground."

BGEN Searby's aid

EDMUND W. SEARBY
BRIG GEN DIV ARTY 80 DIV
CALIFORNIA SEPT 14 1944

THEODORE ROOSEVELT JR
BRIGADIER GENERAL   U S ARMY
NEW YORK   JULY 12 1944

MEDA

When asked what was the bravest thing he ever witnessed, GEN Omar Bradley replied, "Ted Roosevelt on Utah Beach."

FLAG OFFICER WHO LANDED ON D-DAY

BGEN Theodore Roosevelt, Jr., USA
July 12, 1944
Normandy American Cemetery

Teddy Roosevelt, Jr., was the oldest son of former President Theodore Roosevelt. He graduated from Harvard College in 1909 and married Eleanor Butler Alexander in 1910. They had four children: Grace, Theodore, Cornelius, and Quentin (named for Teddy's brother who was killed in WWI). As America prepared for World War I, Teddy completed officer training in New York in 1917 along with his brother, Archibald, and was commissioned an Army Major. He fought with the 1st Division during the Battle of Cantigny and the Battle of Soissons (France), and was injured three times during the Great War. As a Major, he reportedly purchased combat boots for his battalion out of his own pocket. His concern for his troops and his style of leading from the front was evident from his early days as an Army officer. After the war, he was instrumental in creating the American Legion for war veterans.

In 1928-29, he organized a zoological expedition to Asia with his brother, Kermit, to identify native animal species. Upon his return, he served as Assistant Secretary of the Navy, before as Governor of Puerto Rico and of the Philippines. He also worked as a Vice President of Doubleday Books and as Chairman of American Express while serving as an Army Reservist. Shortly after returning to active duty in April 1941, he was promoted to Brigadier General. In the autumn of 1942, he led the 26th Infantry Regiment, 1st Division ashore at Oran, Algeria, during Operation Torch. He was Assistant Commander of the 1st Infantry during the Invasion of Sicily in the summer of 1943. He is perhaps best known for his landing on D-Day: the oldest man and only Army general to land in the first wave, he crisscrossed Utah Beach instilling courage in the men amidst the chaos and bloodshed of the Normandy invasion. GEN Omar Bradley, Commander of the 1st Army at Normandy, requested a battlefield promotion for Roosevelt to Major General and nominated him for the Medal of Honor. Unfortunately, he died of a heart attack on July 12, leaving his widow, Eleanor, to receive his Medal of Honor in September 1944. The Roosevelts (Ted / Teddy Jr.) along with Arthur and Douglas MacArthur are the only father-son pairings to receive the Medals of Honor.

FOUR-STAR GENERAL

GEN George Patton, USA
December 21, 1945
Luxembourg American Cemetery

One of America's greatest warriors, GEN George Patton was both a World War I and World War II hero. As part of the Meuse-Argonne offensive, he was shot in the leg during a daring attack on German machine guns for which he later received the Purple Heart Medal. During the interwar years, he became the driving force in building and training America's armored divisions.

GEN Patton's many achievements during World War II include chasing the Nazis out of North Africa and through Sicily at the start of American aggression; sweeping his Third Army from Brittany to Lorraine after D-Day; and rescuing the 101st Airborne (Easy Company) from encirclement at Bastogne in the Battle of the Bulge.

Patton was born into a wealthy family near Los Angeles. He attended Virginia Military Institute and then the United States Military Academy at West Point, and received his commission in 1909. He married Beatrice Banning Ayer in Massachusetts in 1910, and they had three children: Beatrice, Ruth, and George (IV).

At the 1912 Olympics, Patton finished fifth in the Modern Pentathlon, qualifying for the same event at the canceled 1916 Olympics. He also enjoyed playing polo and sailing. In 1939, he had a schooner built which he named "When and If," saying he would sail it "when and if" he made it home from the war. Instead, Patton died from injuries sustained in an Army vehicle crash in Bavaria just a few months after hostilities ended in 1945. He was 60 years old.

"He was one of those men born to be a soldier, an ideal combat leader. It is no exaggeration to say that Patton's name struck terror at the hearts of the enemy."

GEN Dwight Eisenhower

GEORGE S. PATTON JR
GENERAL THIRD ARMY
CALIFORNIA DEC 21 1945

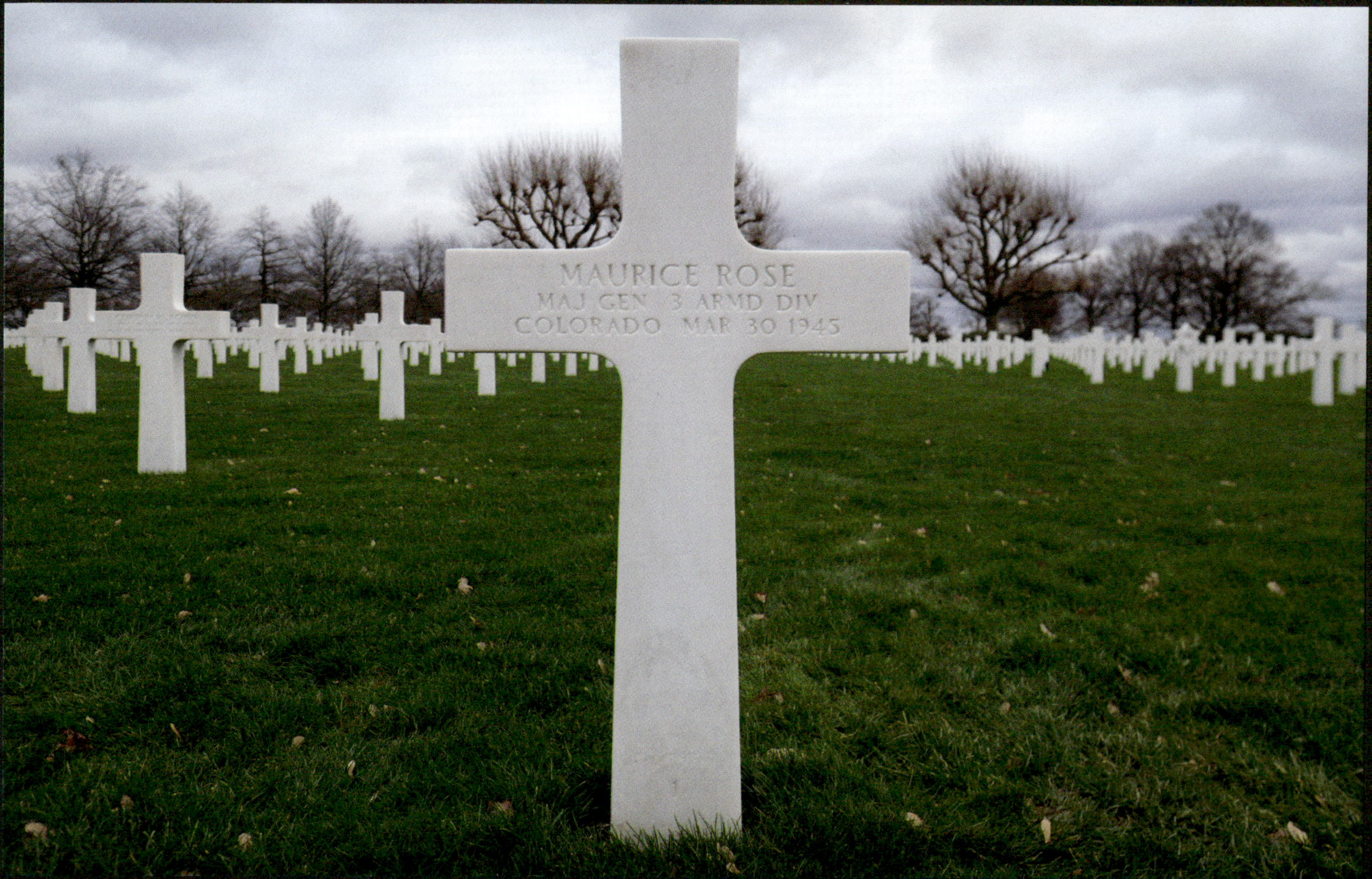
MAURICE ROSE
MAJ GEN 3 ARMD DIV
COLORADO MAR 30 1945

HIGHEST RANKING OFFICER KIA IN EUROPE

MG Maurice Rose, USA
March 30, 1945
Luxembourg American Cemetery

Major General Maurice Rose believed that he needed to be at the front to encourage his men, to understand the battle, to make the best possible decisions, and to minimize casualties.

The son of Polish immigrants, Rose spent most of his youth living in Denver, CO. His father was a rabbi there for more than four decades. Rose left high school in 1916 and was commissioned an Army officer in 1917. As a 19-year-old Lieutenant, he was injured in combat during the St. Mihiel offensive. After the war, he returned briefly to civilian life and worked as a salesman for a mining company, but rejoined the Army in 1920.

Rose had one brother, Arnold, and was married twice, fathering a son in each marriage. He served in armored units during World War II, including America's first offensives in North Africa. He was promoted to Brigadier General and led the 2nd Armored Division ashore at Sicily. He landed with the armored units at Normandy on June 7, 1944, the day after D-Day, and was promoted again to Major General when he was given command of the 3rd Armored Division in August 1944. He led the 3rd Armored Division as they pushed the Nazis out of Belgium, crossed into Germany, and breached the famed Siegfried Line of defense. Over the winter, Rose led his tanks into combat at the Battle of the Bulge and defeated the Nazis at Cologne (Germany).

On March 29, 1945, Rose led the largest single-day advance of any Allied divisions (over 100 miles). The following day he was killed when his jeep encountered a group of German tanks while trying to reach one of his units that was reportedly cut off by enemy forces near Paderborn, Germany. He was shot 14 times while the other members of his group escaped into the nearby woods. Maurice Rose was 45 years old.

USCG ESCORT HIT BY TORPEDO

LT Jonathan Grout, USCG
FIREMAN 1ST CLASS Joseph Hoodock, Jr., USCG
SEAMAN 1ST CLASS, Boyce Nichols, USCG
May 3, 1944
North Africa American Cemetery

Thirty-one men were killed and 25 were injured when a German U-boat torpedoed the recently commissioned USS Menges while on escort duty off the coast of Algeria on May 3, 1944. The ship's commanding officer, LCDR Frank McCabe, USCG, refused to abandon ship despite several explosions that destroyed one-third of the vessel and at least one torpedo on board that went on a hot run. Through the heroic efforts of the crew, the ship was saved and towed to Bougie, Algeria. Later it was towed back to New York, where its hull was melded to the damaged USS Holder, and the ship returned to service just five months later.

Among the crew that perished in May 1944 were LT Jonathan Grout, Fireman 1st Class Joseph Hoodock, and Seaman 1st Class Boyce Ray Nichols. Jonathan Grout attended Princeton University and married Nancy Ferris in 1943 and they lived together in Connecticut. His father was a lawyer and a former judge of the Fairfield Town Court (CT) who passed away in 1942. Before joining the Coast Guard, Grout worked at Bridgeport Fabrics. He was survived by his wife, Nancy, mother, Alice, and two younger brothers, Philip and Thomas, who were both in the service at the time of his death. LT Grout was a direct descendent of COL Jonathan Grout of the First United States Congress (VT). Joseph Hoodock enlisted in January 1943. Before the war, he worked at the Charles T. Main Engineering Corporation. He was a graduate of the Pierre DuPont High School in Delaware, and had been an altar boy at his home parish of Christ Our King Catholic Church. He was survived by his father and his sister. Boyce Ray Nichols lived in Texas and graduated from Albany High School where he was involved in the metal shop program. He was survived by his parents, Boyce and Irene Nichols.

JONATHAN DEWITT GROUT
LIEUTENANT USCG
CONNECTICUT MAY 3 1944

BOYCE RAY NICHOLS
S1C USCG
TEXAS MAY 3 1944

JOSEPH LAWRENCE HOODOCK JR
F1C USCG
DELAWARE MAY 3 1944

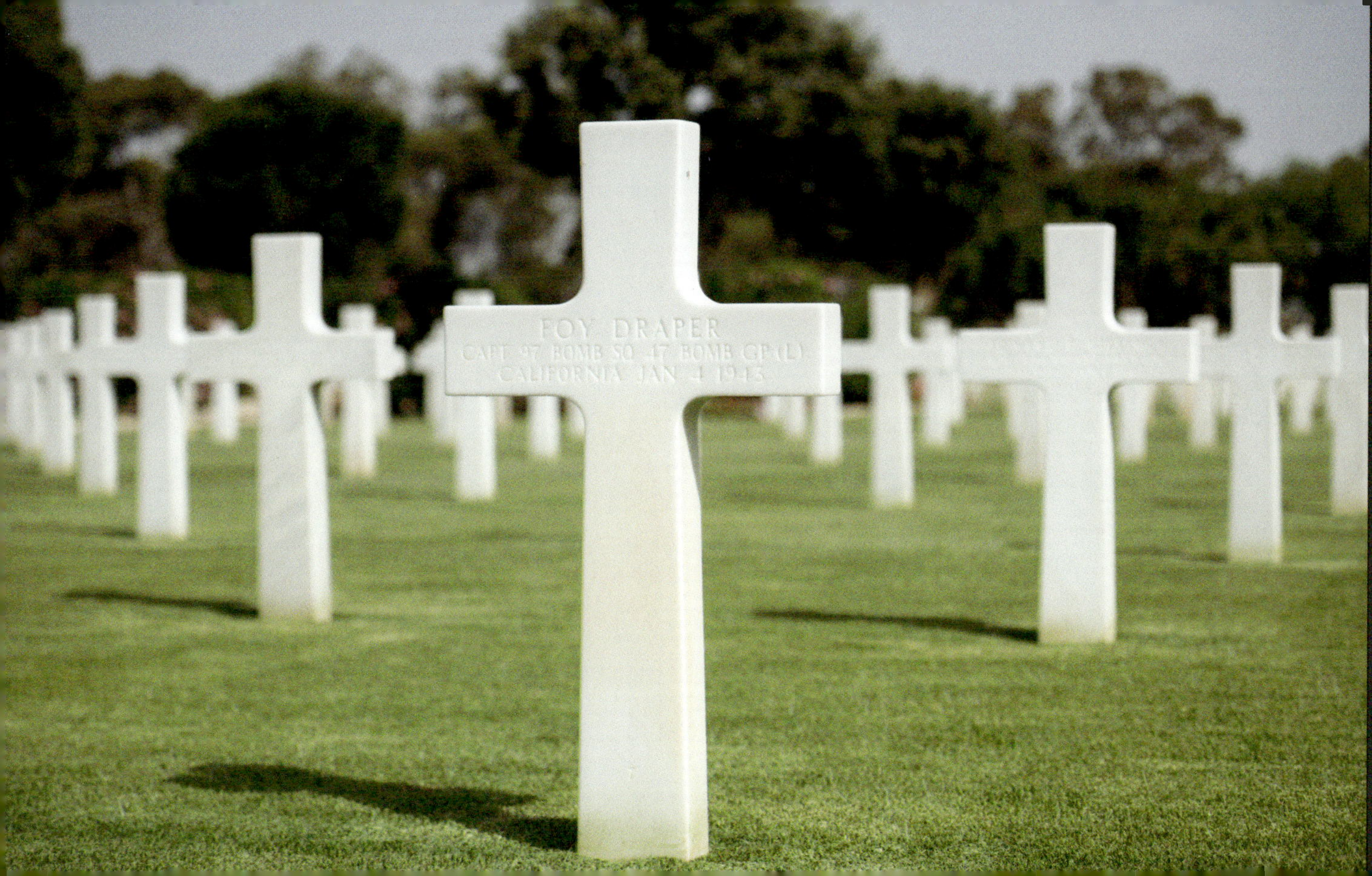
FOY DRAPER
CAPT 97 BOMB SQ 47 BOMB GP (L)
CALIFORNIA JAN 4 1943

OLYMPIC GOLD MEDALIST

CAPT Foy Draper, USAAF
January 4, 1943
North Africa American Cemetery

In 1911, Foy Draper was born in Georgetown, TX, where he lived with his three brothers and parents, David and Bessie Draper. The family moved to California when his older brother, Weldon, was recruited as a sprinter at the University of Southern California (USC).

Draper followed his brother to USC where he held the record in the 220-yard dash and finished second to Jesse Owens in the 1935 collegiate championships in the 100-yard dash. He was president of his senior class at USC (1936) and captain of the track team. He also excelled academically and was part of the Phi Beta Kappa Honor Society. After graduation, Draper went to Berlin where he ran the third leg of America's Olympic gold-medal winning 4x100 relay team that included Jesse Owens. He worked for several years as a school teacher in Inglewood, CA, and married Margaret Marsh in 1941. That same year, his father, David Draper, a preacher and teacher, passed away.

He joined the Army and became a pilot of the A-20B Havoc twin-engine attack bomber. He deployed to Thelepte, Tunisia as part of the 47th Bomb Group, 97th Bomb Squadron in the fall of 1942. On January 4, 1943, CAPT Draper and two crew members took off to participate in the Battle of Kasserine Pass when their plane was lost. Foy Draper was 31 years old.

THREE BROTHERS

SGT Robert Tester, USA
November 26, 1943

SGT James Tester, USA
September 17, 1944

PFC Glenn Tester, USA
January 9, 1945
Henri-Chapelle American Cemetery

There are 38 pairs of brothers interred in Henri-Chapelle American Cemetery, but only one set of three brothers–Robert (Dent), James (Earle), and Glenn* Tester. To lose a family member in service to our nation is unbearable, but the grief for Eliza Tester to have lost three sons to war is incomprehensible. In 1942, Mrs. Tester's husband, Millard, succumbed to cancer and her son, Thomas, died of a heart condition. Then, in 1943, her youngest son, Carroll, received the first of three telegrams from the Army that was sent to the Tester's hometown in eastern Tennessee. The family's oldest son, Robert "Dent" Tester had been killed when his transport ship was sunk off the coast of Tunisia in November. His body later washed ashore in Algeria. Dent had worked as a farmer and woodworker before the war.

James "Earle" Tester, the youngest of the brothers to serve, survived D-Day on Utah Beach, but died in combat a few months later as his unit approached the famed Siegfried Line in Germany. Before the war, he worked for the Civilian Conservation Corps.

The last to perish was Glenn, who was married (Marie) with a three-month-old son (Frank) when he was deployed to Italy in 1944. Glenn received the Purple Heart Medal for injuries sustained in the Italian Campaign. He died in the Vosges Mountains (France) while attached to the 142nd Infantry Regiment, 36th Division. He was 27 years old.

Glenn is the spelling provided by the family

SGT Robert Tester

SGT James Tester

PFC Glenn Tester

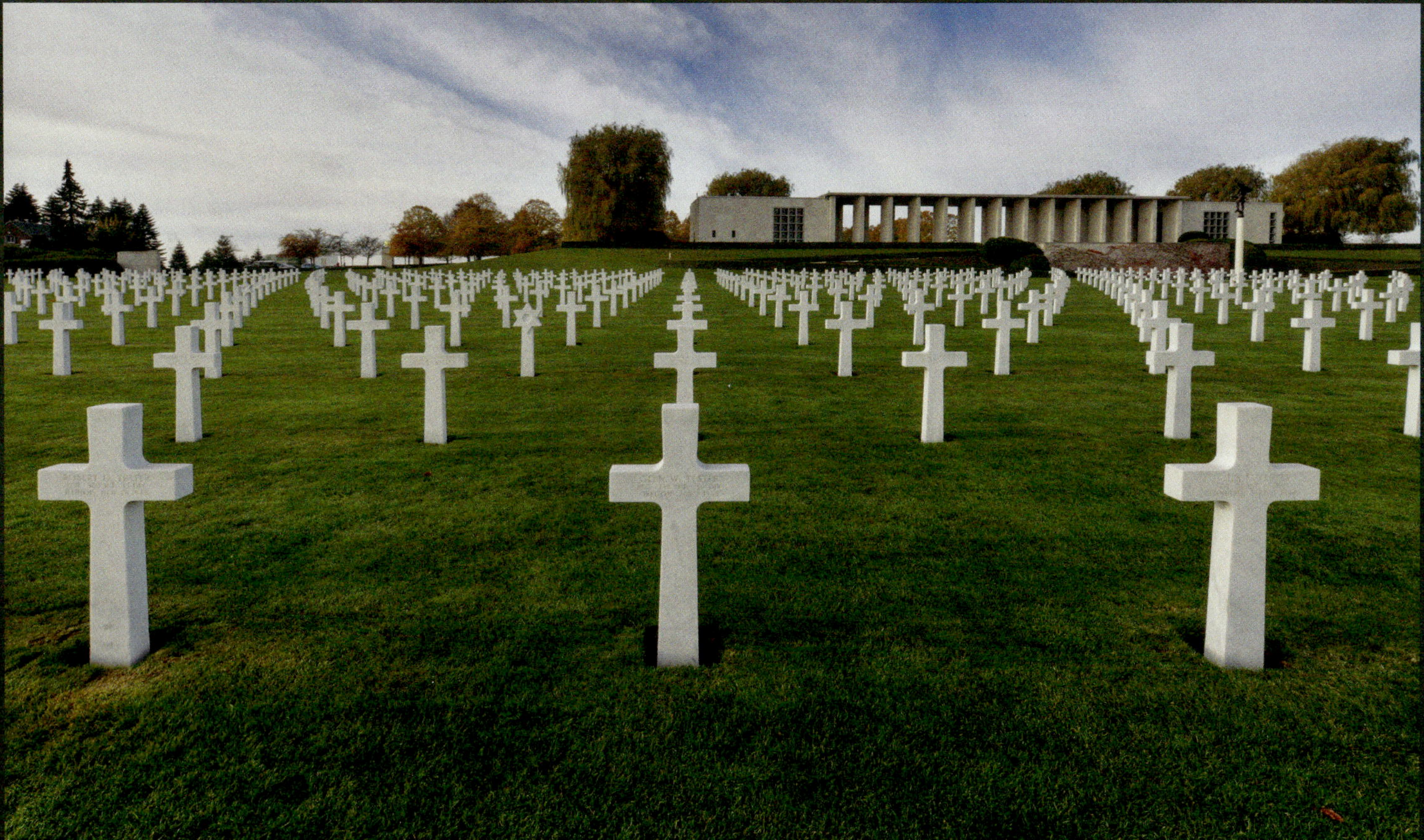

GOODMAN BROTHERS

2LT Sanford Goodman, USA
November 30, 1944

SSGT Elliott Goodman, USA
May 17, 1945
Netherlands American Cemetery

Elliott and Sanford Goodman grew up in Cleveland Heights, OH. Their father, Louis, was an immigrant from Austria-Hungary who spoke German and worked as a barber in town. They had an older brother, Mortimer, and a younger sister, Ellen, and lived in a two-floor house on shady Coventry Road. Elliott finished high school and worked as a salesman for United Linoleum Company. He enlisted in February 1943, almost two years after his younger brother, Sanford. Elliott was only 5'2" but served in the Army's Quartermaster Corps. He never married and died just nine days after VE day while still serving in Europe.

Sanford ("Sandy") also worked in sales and was employed at Godin Carpet in Cleveland Heights before joining the Army. He married Sarah "Sadie" Silver of North Carolina during his Army training before deploying to Europe. He enlisted in June 1941 and, by 1944, had become an Army officer. He served as a Second Lieutenant with the 84th Infantry Division, but was killed in fighting near Lindern, Germany in November 1944.

2LT Sanford Goodman

SSGT Elliott Goodman

ROOSEVELT BROTHERS

1LT Quentin Roosevelt, USA
July 14, 1918

BGEN Theodore Roosevelt, Jr., USA
July 12, 1944
Normandy American Cemetery

Quentin Roosevelt, the youngest son of former President Theodore Roosevelt, was a daring pilot with the 95th Aero Squadron in an era when pilot life expectancy was measured in weeks. He recorded at least one confirmed kill during his service in World War I, but died in aerial combat over German-occupied Chamery (France) just four days later in the Second Battle of the Marne. Upon identifying the dead American pilot, the Germans buried Quentin with full battlefield honors at the site of the crash. An American POW who witnessed the event reported that an estimated 1,000 German troops paid their respects to the enemy pilot. LT Edward Buford, the flight leader on that mission, said of Quentin:

> "His loss was one of the severest blows we have ever had in the squadron, but he certainly died fighting."

For his heroic actions, he was awarded France's Croixe de Guerre. Quentin's body remained in Chamery until 1955 when it was moved to the Normandy American Cemetery. He is interred next to his eldest brother, Theodore Roosevelt, Jr. Quentin Roosevelt remains the only child of a US president to die in combat; he was 20 years old.

"The aviator of the American Squadron, Quentin Roosevelt, in trying to break through the air zone over the Marne, met the death of a hero."

Kölnische Zeitung/Cologne Newspaper via Spanish Embassy

83

MITSULU E. MIYOKO
T SGT 100 BN 442 INF REGT
CALIFORNIA OCT 15 1944

NOBORU MIYOKO
PFC 442 INF 106 DIV
CALIFORNIA APR 14 1945

JAPANESE AMERICAN BROTHERS

TSGT Mitsulu Miyoko, USA
October 15, 1944
Epinal American Cemetery

PFC Noboru Miyoko, USA
April 14, 1945
Florence American Cemetery

Mitsulu* and Noboru Miyoko came from a Japanese American family of 10 children that lived near Los Angeles, CA. Their brothers, Takeshi and George, also served in the US Army during World War II. Their parents, Masaichiro and Yuka, moved to Japan in 1940 along with two of their sons, Tsutomu and James. After the attacks on Pearl Harbor, the rest of the family moved to Utah to avoid being placed in concentration camps.

Mitsulu entered the Army a few months before the attacks on Pearl Harbor and served with the famed 100th Infantry Battalion/442nd Regimental Combat Team, one of the most decorated combat units in World War II. The unit was comprised mostly of Japanese Americans. Mitsulu was killed during the Battle of Bruyeres in eastern France on October 15, 1944. His brother, Noboru, died six months later on the last day of intense fighting near Castelpoggio, Italy, northwest of Florence. Mitsulu and Noboru were survived by brothers Sam, Takeshi, George, Tsutomu, and James, as well as their sister, Matsue. Mitsulu left behind a wife, Sadako Salki (married in 1940), and Noboru was survived by his wife, Miyuki, and his baby daughter, Susanne, who was born in January 1944. Mitsulu was 30 years old; Noburu was 25.

Mitsulu Miyoko's name sometimes appears as Mitsuru; however, his name is listed as Mitsulu on his draft card and headstone.

TSGT Mitsulu Miyoko

PFC Noboru Miyoko

FIVE MISSING BROTHERS

GM2 George Sullivan, USN
SN2 Joseph Sullivan, USN
SN2 Albert Sullivan, USN
SN2 Madison Sullivan, USN
COX Francis Sullivan, USN
November 13, 1942
Manila American Cemetery

On January 3, 1942, the five Sullivan brothers—George, Joseph, Albert, Madison, and Francis—enlisted together after one of their friends was killed aboard the USS Arizona at Pearl Harbor. Their one requirement was they be allowed to serve aboard the same ship. Before the year was over, all five would be dead.

George and Francis had recently completed service in the Navy aboard the destroyer USS Hovey before reenlisting.

The five brothers deployed on the light cruiser USS Juneau which moved to the Pacific fleet in August 1942. During the Battle of Guadalcanal, the ship was hit by a torpedo and sunk in 42 seconds.

At 27 years of age, George was the oldest of the brothers and survived the longest. However, he reportedly jumped into the sea when he learned all his brothers had perished. Even after the loss of the sons, the family remained active in helping to sell war bonds. Two Navy ships were subsequently named to honor the Sullivans.

SULLIVAN	ALBERT LEO	SEAMAN 2C	USNR	IOWA
SULLIVAN	CALVIN C	SEAMAN 1C	USNR	MISSOURI
SULLIVAN	CHARLES F	LIEUTENANT (JG)	USNR	ILLINOIS
SULLIVAN	DAVID J	SEAMAN 2C	USN	ILLINOIS
SULLIVAN	DONALD L	SIGNALMAN 2C	USN	MAINE
SULLIVAN	EARL P	SEAMAN 1C	USNR	ARKANSAS
SULLIVAN	EDWARD F JR	LIEUTENANT (JG)	USNR	WISCONSIN
SULLIVAN	EUGENE F	SEAMAN 2C	USNR	NEW JERSEY
SULLIVAN	FRANCIS H	COXSWAIN	USNR	IOWA
SULLIVAN	FRANCIS M	FIRE CONTROLMAN 3C	USNR	MAINE
SULLIVAN	GEORGE B	GUNNER'S MATE 3C	USN	RHODE ISLAND
SULLIVAN	GEORGE T	GUNNER'S MATE 2C	USNR	IOWA
SULLIVAN	GERALD M JR	LIEUTENANT	USNR	MASSACHUSETTS
SULLIVAN	HAROLD W	FIREMAN 1C	USNR	ILLINOIS
SULLIVAN	HUGH D	SEAMAN 1C	USNR	GEORGIA
SULLIVAN	HUGH E	CHIEF MTR MACHINIST'S MATE	USN	N H
SULLIVAN	JAMES P	SEAMAN 2C	USNR	MICHIGAN
SULLIVAN	JOHN EDWARD	SEAMAN 1C	USN	MASSACHUSETTS
SULLIVAN	JOHN J JR	ELECTRICIAN'S MATE 3C	USNR	MASSACHUSETTS
SULLIVAN	JOSEPH E	SEAMAN 2C	USNR	IOWA
SULLIVAN	KENNETH J	AVN MACHINIST'S MATE 3C	USNR	MASS
SULLIVAN	KENNETH LEE	STOREKEEPER 3C	USN	KENTUCKY
SULLIVAN	LEON J	CHIEF GUNNER'S MATE	USN	CALIFORNIA
SULLIVAN	MADISON A	SEAMAN 2C	USNR	IOWA
SULLIVAN	ROBERT A	FIREMAN 2C	USNR	NEW YORK
SULLIVAN	THOMAS J	SIGNALMAN 1C	USN	TEXAS

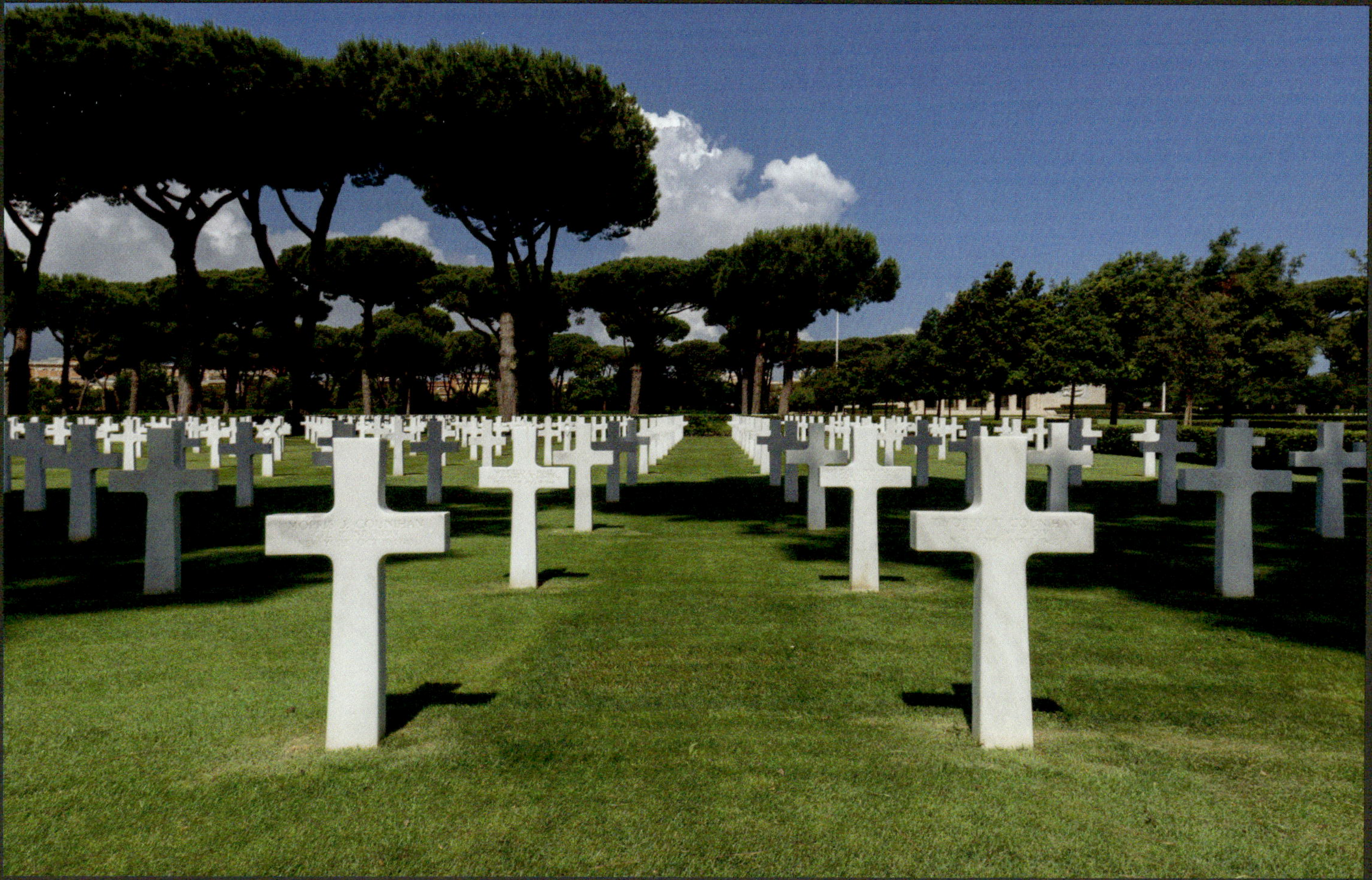

TWIN BROTHERS

PVT Timothy Counihan, USA
April 7, 1943

CPL Morrison Counihan, USA
October 18, 1943
Sicily-Rome American Cemetery

Twin brothers, Timothy and Morris Counihan, were born on July 6, 1919, and lived in Brooklyn, NY. After completing grade school, the twins worked various jobs in town. Timothy worked for the well-known Germains department store in Brooklyn. In September 1940, the brothers decided to join the Army before the draft began and they trained together at Fort Dix, NJ. Their older brother, John, also served in the Army.

In 1943, the twins shipped off to North Africa. Timothy was part of the 47th Infantry Regiment, 9th Division. In April, he was killed by machine-gun fire as the Americans defeated the Italian and German forces (notably the 10th Panzer Division) during the Battle of El Guettar in Tunisia.

The month after Timothy was killed, Morris was hit in the shoulder by shrapnel and hospitalized in North Africa (likely Morocco). He returned to his unit and crossed the Mediterranean Sea with the 15th Infantry Regiment, 3th Infantry Division. In October 1943, his unit battled across the well-defended and rain-swollen Volturno River near Naples (Italy), but Morris was killed by a shell fragment.

Irish immigrants, Timothy and Catherine Counihan, had lost their twin sons in a span of just six months.

EASY COMPANY/THE "BAND OF BROTHERS"

SGT Warren H. Muck, USA
PFC Alex M. Penkala, Jr., USA
January 10, 1945
Luxembourg American Cemetery

Warren Muck and Alex Penkala, Jr., were part of a mortar squad with the elite 101st Airborne Division. They were assigned to "Easy Company" of the 506th Parachute Infantry Regiment (PIR) made famous by Stephen Ambrose's book and TV series "Band of Brothers." Easy Company landed behind Utah Beach just after midnight on D-Day in June 1944. They then parachuted into Holland and later traveled over land to Bastogne (Belgium) for the frigid Battle of the Bulge, where they defended this key town despite being severely outnumbered, under-equipped, and surrounded by the enemy. During the 11 months of combat operations, Easy Company suffered a 150% casualty rate, leaving few of the original men still fighting by war's end. Skip Muck and Alex Penkala never made it to VE Day. They died when a mortar shell fell onto their foxhole in the Battle of Bois Jacques (Belgium) in January 1945.

Alex Penkala, Jr., was one of 12 children born to Alexander and Mary Penkala. His parents were immigrants and the family spoke Polish in their home located near Notre Dame University. Mary had 12 children, but died in childbirth when Alex was just four years old. Alex's father and his older sisters raised the family after her death. Penkala dropped out of high school and enlisted in February 1943 at the age of 18. He worked as an Army cook before joining the elite paratroopers.

Warren Muck was a high-energy kid growing up in Tonawanda, NY, when he got his nickname "Skip" for his preferred ambulation style. He graduated from Tonawanda High School in 1941, where he was a member of the swim team and played wide receiver on the football team. He once swam the fast-flowing Niagara River and survived. He had a younger sister, Ruth, and an older brother, Elmer. In high school, Muck worked as a paperboy, at a hot dog stand, and then for the Remington Rand Corporation before joining the Army.

He was one of the best-liked men in Easy Company. In an interview years later, 1SGT Les Hashey, one of Muck's PIR colleagues said, "We all loved him."

"The Muck and Penkala families are close even today, more than 60 years later."

Rudolph Tatay, Alex Penkala, Jr.'s, nephew in *A Company of Heroes* (2010)

91

HELEN FAIRCHILD
NURSE BASE HOSPITAL 10 A.N.C.
PENNSYLVANIA JAN. 18, 1918

NURSE

Helen Fairchild, USA Nurse Corps
January 18, 1918
Somme American Cemetery

You can't measure courage in inches or pounds. Just 5'2" and 122 pounds, Helen Fairchild volunteered for the US Army Reserve Nurse Corps in 1917. Just four years after graduating from the Pennsylvania Hospital in Philadelphia, she arrived in France in May 1917 to staff the first of six "Base Hospitals" created by the American Red Cross to care for the British Expeditionary Forces. In June 1917, her team took over Base Hospital 10 located near the coastal city of Le Tréport, France. A few weeks later, she volunteered to forward deploy to Casualty Clearing Station #4, north of Ypres (Belgium) during the famous Third Battle of Ypres (also referred to as "Passchendaele"). She spent the summer and autumn of 1917 near the front, where she was exposed repeatedly to bombardment and mustard gas. It is documented that she gave her gas mask to an injured soldier on at least one occasion. In her letters home, she described her team digging below the medical tents to protect themselves from the bombardment, and lamented the "re-wounding and killing of already wounded men."

Helen was one of seven children, born to Ambrose and Adda Fairchild in Milton, PA. Her letters home reveal her energetic, can-do personality:

> *"Gee but I'll be glad to see you all by the time this war is over, but at the same time I am glad to be here to help take care of these poor [British] men, and I'll be doubly glad when our own US boys will be...with us."*

Ms. Fairchild was among the first US Army nurses to die in the Great War. She was 33 years old.

FLIGHT NURSE

1LT Wilma Vinsant, USAAF
April 14, 1945
Netherlands American Cemetery

By mid-April 1945, the war was over for Wilma Vinsant. A flight nurse from San Benito, TX, she had completed all her required missions and had earned her ticket home. She spent nearly three years as part of the 806th Medical Air Evacuation Squadron (MAES) that brought wounded soldiers back to hospitals in England and the US. On April 14th, she requested permission for one more flight so that one of her fellow nurses, Dolores Rike, could go to a party. The C-47 Dakota that carried Wilma Vinsant on her final flight crashed over Germany, killing all six crew members aboard.

Vinsant enlisted on September 1, 1942, exactly 25 years after her father, Dr. William Vinsant joined the Army to serve as a doctor in World War I. She qualified with the first class of flight nurses for the US Army Air Force in February 1943. She was then sent to England to train for and support the US offensives in Europe, including D-Day. In early 1945, she married US Army MAJ Walter Shea in Berkshire, England, and then celebrated her 28th birthday on February 17, 1945.

April 1945 was a busy month for the 806th MAES, with more than 17,000 troops evacuated by the squadron. Vinsant is one of 17 Army flight nurses to have died on active duty in Europe during World War II.

WILMA R. VINSANT
1 LT 806 AIR EVAC SQ
TEXAS   APR 14 1945

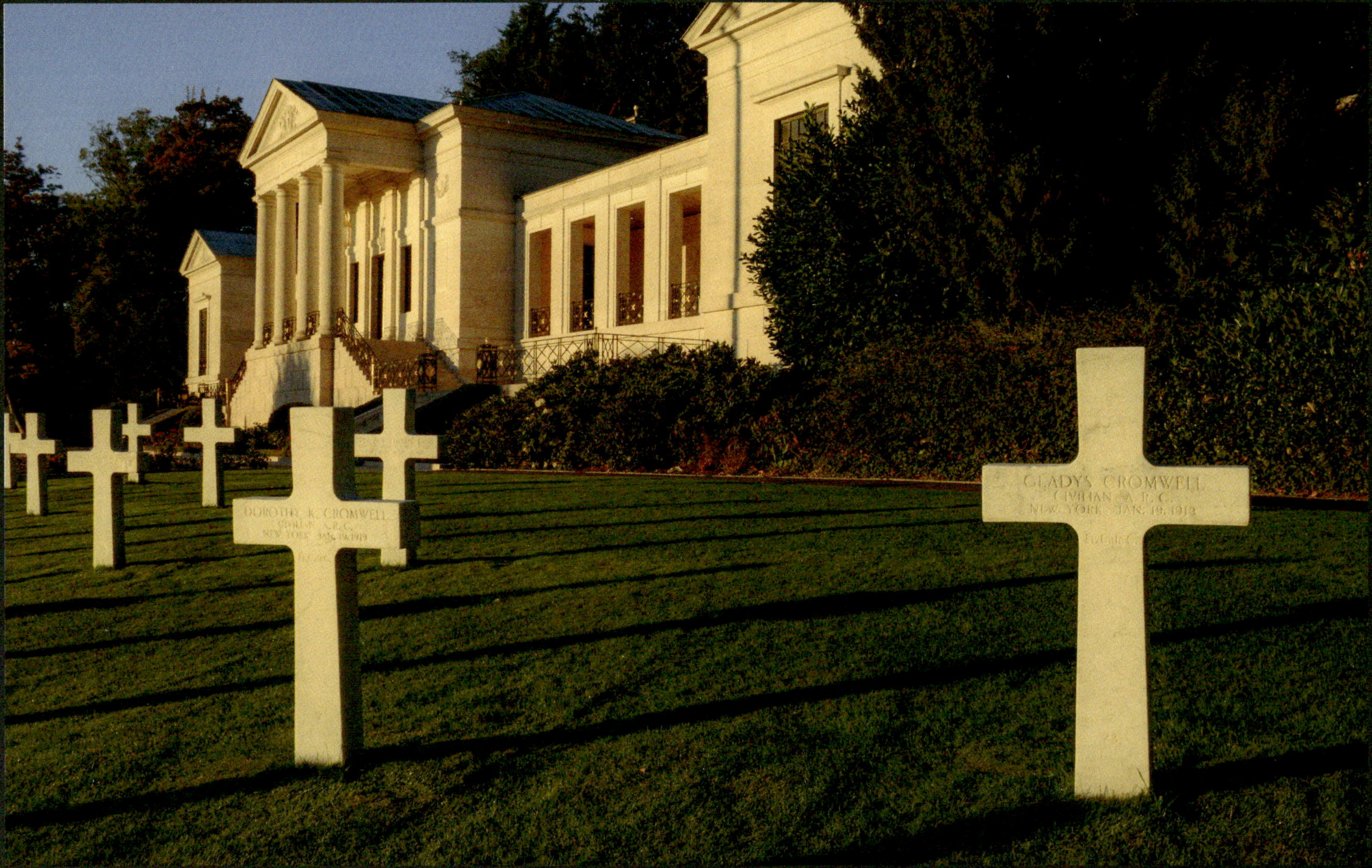
GLADYS CROMWELL

TWIN SISTERS

Dorothy & Gladys Cromwell, Red Cross
January 19, 1919
Suresnes American Cemetery

Dorothy* and Gladys Cromwell, twin sisters from a wealthy New York family, departed for Europe as volunteers in the Red Cross canteen service in January 1918. Soon thereafter, they arrived at Chalons-sur-Marne (France), where the French soldiers called them "Twin Angels." After eight months, the sisters requested to work with American troops and were sent to an evacuation hospital in Verdun, where they worked in canteen and hospital services even after the war's end. After extended service on the front without rest, they were finally convinced by their brother to return home in January 1919, three months after the Armistice. Suspected now to have suffered from post-traumatic stress disorder (PTSD), the Cromwell twins committed suicide by leaping from the steamship La Lorraine shortly after it departed Bordeaux for home in January 1919.

Their bodies were recovered on March 20, 1919. Two days later, the sisters—who were born on the same day and died on the same date—were awarded the Croixe de Guerre, a medal awarded for gallantry in war by France.

Dorothy Cromwell's name sometimes appears as "Dorothea"

NURSE

Teresa Murphy, USA Nurse Corps
November 9, 1918
Brookwood American Cemetery

Teresa Margaret Murphy was born on October 31, 1891, in County Amagh, Ireland, and was one of six children. At 19, she emigrated to the United States, arriving in Boston in August 1910. Upon completing her studies in nursing, she worked and lived as a registered nurse in New Hampshire and became a US citizen in 1916. A petite 5'3" and 105 pounds, she joined America's war effort. Records indicate she arrived in Europe by February 1918. The entire scope of her duties is undocumented, but her final location was a hospital in England that treated those suffering from pulmonary tuberculosis. While helping those stricken with this contagious disease, she contracted tuberculosis and died in London on November 9, 1918, just two days before the Armistice that ended the Great War.

TERESA M. MURPHY
NURSE HDQRS. BASE SEC. 3 A.N.C.
NEW HAMPSHIRE NOV. 9, 1918

HAZEL M. BINGNER
TEC 5 NEW GUINEA BASE SEC
DISTRICT OF COLUMBIA MAY 15 1945

FEMALE TECH SERGEANT IN THE FAR EAST

TSGT Hazel Bingner, USA
May 15, 1945
Manila American Cemetery

Hazel Marie Bingner was hospitalized several times for illness while serving as a Technician Fifth Class in the US Army in the Pacific Theatre. Born in September 1917 in Marquette, MI, Bingner joined the Army in February 1943, after completing a year of business studies at Bob Jones College in Cleveland, TN. While there, she was a member of the Chi Sigma Phi sorority.

As part of the Women's Army Corps (WAC), she spent the fall of 1943 in Washington, DC, and, while stationed there, participated in radio bible quizzes. She worked as a stenographer/typist while in the WAC and died in Oro Bay, New Guinea, on May 15, 1945. She was survived by her parents, Frank and Ella, as well as a brother and sister. Hazel Bingner was 27 years old.

AFS AMBULANCE DRIVER

Vernon Preble, Civilian
December 1, 1943
Sicily-Rome American Cemetery

Vernon Preble volunteered for the American Field Service (AFS) during World War II. His father, Elwin, served in the US Army during World War I. In 1920, Elwin married Bessie, a young woman who had immigrated from Canada in 1912. In February 1921, they had twins—Vernon and his sister, Thais. In 1927, Elwin passed away and Bessie moved the family to Massachusetts, where Vernon attended Lowell High School.

Preble worked as an ambulance driver in World War II. American four-wheel ambulances were in great demand, as they could handle the muddy conditions that prevailed in theatre. In 1942, Preble worked in Egypt in support of the British Army. In December 1943, he was in Italy with the British 8th Army ferrying injured soldiers to aid stations from the front. Preble was killed when his ambulance struck a mine along the Sangro River, north of Naples. He was posthumously awarded the Oak Leaf Emblem for distinguished service by the British Army.

VERNON W. PREBLE
AMERICAN FIELD SERVICE
MASSACHUSETTS DEC 1 1943

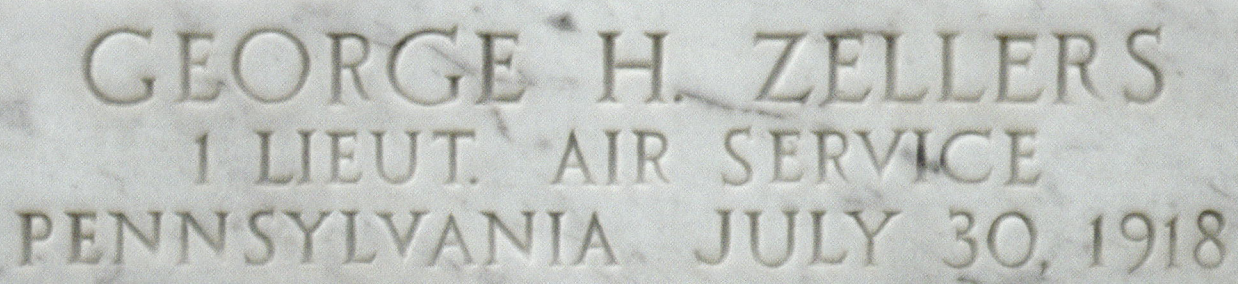

GEORGE H. ZELLERS
1 LIEUT. AIR SERVICE
PENNSYLVANIA   JULY 30, 1918

WWI PILOT FOR ROYAL AIR FORCE

1LT George Zellers, USA
July 30, 1918
Flanders Field American Cemetery

George Zellers was a biology teacher at Hazleton High School (PA) for a year, but decided to volunteer for the US "Aerial Forces" in June 1917. He was commissioned in August that year, and then received aviation training at Ohio State University and later on Long Island. His training continued with the Royal Air Force (RAF) at Oxford (England) and in Ayres, Scotland. Upon completion of his training, he was assigned to the 20th Squadron of the RAF.

Zellers was a graduate of Franklin and Marshall College, where he received his undergraduate and graduate degrees in Biology, and was a member of the Phi Sigma Kappa fraternity. His father was a Reverend in the Episcopal Church. He had five siblings, including an older brother, John Herbert Zellers, who died of the Spanish Flu just a few months after George was killed.

On July 30, 1918, Zellers' aircraft along with 11 other RAF aircraft engaged approximately 30 German aircraft over Germany. LT Zellers and his observer are credited with having shot down two enemy aircraft before being killed in action by enemy gunfire. Zellers' body was recovered by British infantry units along the front in Belgium. George Zellers was 25 years old.

"War knows no holidays or holy days."
LT George Zellers in a letter home, 1918

WORLD WAR I AVIATOR

1LT George Preston Glenn, USA
July 20, 1918
Flanders Field American Cemetery

George Preston Glenn was born on June 21, 1894, the son of Walter and Mary Glenn of Lynchburg, VA. Mary died when George was 14 years old, and his father, who had worked as a telegraph operator, passed away when George was 20 years old. George enlisted in May 1917, and soon became an officer assigned to the 17th and 23rd Aero Squadrons. He was shot down by German Fokkers near Ostend (Belgium) after escorting bombers in an attack on Bruges. It is unclear whether he died immediately in the attack. George was survived by an older brother and sister, as well as a younger brother. In a letter to his sister, Blanche, one of his fellow fighter pilots wrote:

> *"'I regret very much to tell you that [Glenn] had a little hard luck today while on patrol over Hunland. A Hun got behind him and he evidently did not see him. The Hun opened fire, and [Glenn] first pulled his machine up, and then did a long, low dive.... [He] did not return home, and nothing had been heard from him. He very probably landed in Hunland and is a prisoner."*

GEORGE PRESTON GLENN
1 LIEUT 17 AERO SQDN
VIRGINIA JULY 20 1918

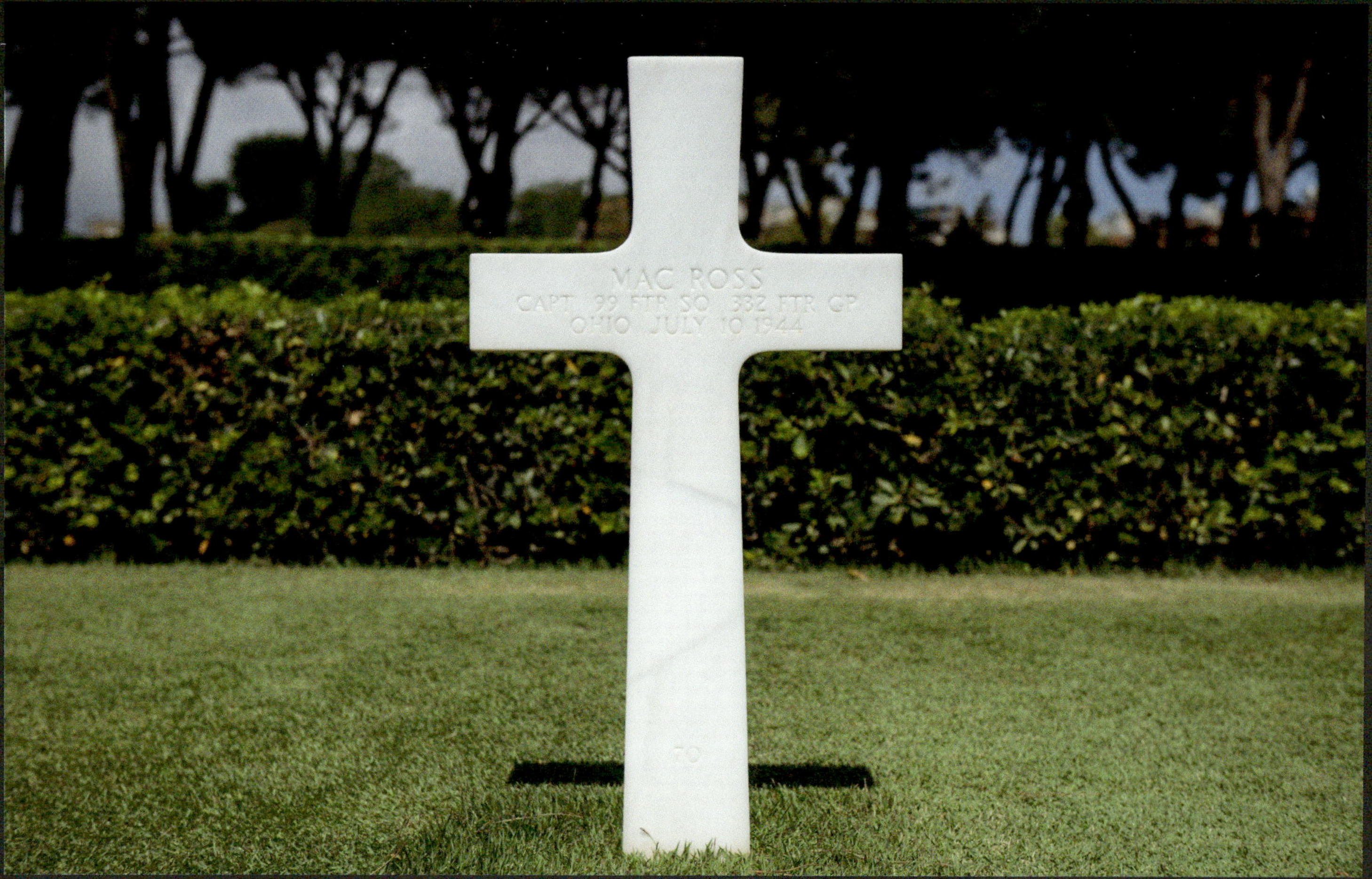
MAC ROSS
CAPT 99 FTR SQ 332 FTR GP
OHIO JULY 10 1944
70

TUSKEGEE AIRMAN

CAPT Mac Ross, USAAF
July 10, 1944
Sicily-Rome American Cemetery

Mac Ross was born in Selma, AL in June 1916. His father, Sam, worked on a farm in Selma before moving the family to Dayton, OH. In his youth, Mac delivered newspapers. He graduated from Roosevelt High School in 1936.

Ross's interest in flying blossomed while he studied at West Virginia State College. He joined their civilian training program for pilots in 1939 and received his private pilot's license the following year along with his college diploma. Following graduation, Ross returned home and worked as an inspector at the Dayton Malleable and Iron Company.

In July 1941, he was accepted as a cadet in the now famous Tuskegee program for Black aviators. He received his Army commission in March 1942 as part of the first class of Black Army pilots. In August, he served as best man in the wedding of his aviation classmate, 2LT Charles H. DeBow, while training in Tuskegee.

In August 1942, he was promoted to commanding officer of the 100th Pursuit Squadron at Tuskegee Airfield. While flying there, he narrowly avoided death when his engine caught fire and exploded. Ross parachuted to safety, becoming the first Black person to join the "Caterpillar" club, a group of aviators who parachuted from a disabled aircraft.

He married LT Abigail Voorhies, an Army nurse also stationed at Tuskegee, on June 3, 1943, and then deployed overseas in December. Ross flew more than 50 combat missions while in Italy and was promoted to Captain in May 1944. On July 10, 1944, he died during a check flight of a new P-51 near Foggia (Italy). He is the highest-ranking Tuskegee Airman interred at Sicily-Rome American Cemetery.

WORLD WAR I AVIATOR

1LT Henry Edgar Fulghum, USA
September 24, 1918
Suresnes American Cemetery

Born in 1898 in Hapeville, GA, Henry was the second oldest of five children born to John and Ava Fulghum. He graduated with honors from Boys' High School in Atlanta and worked briefly for *The Atlanta Journal* in the circulation department, as well as for Southern Railways.

He trained with the Army's newly-formed aviation units at Camp Rich (TX) in 1917 and was commissioned in May 1918. He was assigned to the 103rd Aero Squadron, whose roots trace back to the famed Lafayette Escadrille, the squadron of mostly American volunteer aviators who fought under French command from 1916 to 1918. Henry survived less than five months, dying in an aircraft accident in France, an all too common occurrence during the early days of military aviation.

"There is, of course, an exhilaration in flying. The air is fresh and rushing by... There are only three sources of danger—carelessness, foolishness, and fright. Fright is the most interesting of these."

A letter from LT Henry Fulghum published by the *The Atlanta Journal*, September 13, 1918

111

JOHN HUNTER WIC
2 LIEUT. 353 INF. 8
COLORADO SEPT.

M.H., U.S.A.
ITALY

M
E
D
A
L
of
H
O
N
O
R

AGE: 28
DEATH: Wounds
GOLD STAR PILGRIMAGE: Mother (71)

John Hunter Wickersham

MEDAL OF HONOR

2LT John Hunter Wickersham, USA
September 12, 1918
St. Mihiel American Cemetery

Prior to 1915, only enlisted personnel could receive the Medal of Honor, so John Hunter Wickersham was among the first officers to receive the award. After being wounded in four places by a high-explosive shell at the start of the St. Mihiel (France) offensive, he continued to fight. His Medal of Honor citation described his heroic actions:

"Before receiving any aid for himself he dressed the wounds of his orderly, who was wounded at the same time. He then ordered and accompanied the further advance of his platoon, although weakened by the loss of blood. His right hand and arm being disabled by wounds, he continued to fire his revolver with his left hand until, exhausted by loss of blood, he fell and died from his wounds."

Wickersham authored a poem in his last letter home, which included the stanza:

"An' you just can't help a-figuring–sitting there alone–
About this war and hero stuff and that,
And you wonder if they haven't sort of got things twisted up,
While the rain keeps up its patter on your old tin hat."

BLACK MEDAL OF HONOR – WORLD WAR II

SSGT Ruben Rivers, USA
November 19, 1944
Lorraine American Cemetery

Ruben Rivers was born in October 1918 to Willie and Lillian Rivers and had at least one brother, Dewey, who also served overseas with the Army during World War II. Ruben grew up in Tecumseh, OK, attended Dunbar High School (later integrated into Shawnee High School), and worked on the railroad before the war. He was drafted in 1942.

Ruben was assigned to the "Black Panthers" (the 761st Tank Battalion), a unit comprised exclusively of Black soldiers who served with distinction during World War II under GEN George Patton. After suffering a deep shrapnel wound in fighting near Guebling in northeastern France, Rivers refused medical treatment and evacuation and continued to fight the Germans for another two-and-a-half days. He was killed while exposing his tank to enemy fire in order to cover his unit's retreat near Bougaltroff, France. His Commanding Officer, CAPT David Williams immediately nominated Rivers for the Medal of Honor. Instead, he was awarded the Distinguished Service Cross, the Army's second highest medal. Fifty-three years later, on January 13, 1997, Ruben Rivers' sister, Grace Woodfork, accepted his Medal of Honor from President Bill Clinton. In attendance was his former Commanding Officer, David Williams.

"He pushed the [morphine] needle away and got up. He said. 'This is the one order, the only order, I'll ever disobey.'"

Ruben Rivers refusing medical care and evacuation, as recounted by his Commanding Officer, CAPT David Williams

RUBEN RIVERS
S SGT 761 TK BN
OKLAHOMA NOV 19 1944
MEDAL OF HONOR

WILLIAM SAWELSON
SUP.SGT. 312 INF. 78 DIV.
N. JERSEY OCT. 26. 1918
M.H. U.S.A.
IT. C. DI. G.
MEDAL OF HONOR

MEDAL OF HONOR – WORLD WAR I

SGT William Sawelson, USA
October 26, 1918
Meuse-Argonne American Cemetery

William Sawelson was born in August 1895 in Newark, NJ to Jacob and Golda Sawelson. Prior to the war, he worked as a chauffeur.

Sawelson was a supply sergeant in M Company, 312th Infantry Regiment, 78th Division during the bloody Meuse-Argonne offensive in the autumn of 1918. During the Battle of Grand-Pre (France) in October, Sawelson heard the cries of a wounded soldier from a nearby shell hole. He left the safety of his shelter and took his canteen to the injured man despite heavy machine-gun fire. During the Meuse-Argonne offensive, resources and fresh water were often scarce. Sawelson left the injured man, found more water, and, while returning to his aid, was killed by enemy fire. For his actions, Sawelson was posthumously awarded the Medal of Honor—one of four men of Jewish faith to have received the nation's highest honor for their gallantry in World War I.

After his death, the War Department communicated with the family, and his mother decided that Sawelson should be buried at Arlington National Cemetery. However, she changed her mind and asked that her son be buried with his men. His father, Jacob, received his Medal of Honor. William Sawelson is interred at Meuse-Argonne American Cemetery. He was 23 years old.

MEDAL OF HONOR – NAVY DENTIST

LTJG Weedon E. Osborne, USN
June 6, 1918
Aisne-Marne American Cemetery

LTJG Weedon* Osborne was commissioned a Navy Officer on May 8, 1917. He was a graduate of Northwestern University's Dental School (1915), and had been on the teaching staff at Denver University before the war. According to the *Journal of the National Dental Association*, he had a "slight build, nervous temperament; bright, forceful, energetic, and of sympathetic and lovable disposition."

Osborne earned his medal during the famed Battle of Belleau Wood, where the Marine Corps cemented its reputation for toughness over several weeks of fighting that stopped the German offensive that had brought them within reach of Paris. On July 30, 1918, an enemy shell exploded killing him and CAPT Donald Duncan, an injured Marine he was carrying to safety. Osborne's Commanding Officer later wrote:

> "Having joined this regiment but a few days before, and new to the service, he displayed heroism worthy of its best traditions."

Osborne was 25 years old. His nearest relative, Elizabeth Osborne, attended the launch of DD-295 in 1919, a Navy destroyer named after her brother.

*Weedon Osborne's name appears as Weeden on his headstone; however, all Navy correspondence that I found list his name as Weedon.

WEEDEN E. OSBORNE
LIEUT. J.G. U.S. NAVY
ILLINOIS JUNE 6, 1918
M.H. U.S.N.
D.S.C.
It. C. di G.
MEDAL OF HONOR
39

LOUIS J. VAN SCHAICK
COLONEL U S ARMY
NEW YORK FEB 14 1945
MEDAL of HONOR

"...(T)he man who reaches out for the rights and privileges but neglects the duties is a bad citizen. Good citizens are interested not only in the things which affect themselves, but in the things which affect the community....in which they live."

COL Van Schaick lecturing at Ft. Leavenworth

MOH TO POW

COL Louis Van Schaick, USA
February 14, 1945
Manila American Cemetery

Louis Van Schaick was the son of Frances and John Van Schaick who had six children. He entered the United States Military Academy at West Point as a member of the class of 1900. He was commissioned in 1899 and was sent to the Philippines as part of the 4th Cavalry. In 1901, he received the Medal of Honor for his gallant actions, which included leading a pursuit of enemy forces on horseback and then engaging in hand-to-hand combat during the Filipino Insurrection. 1LT Van Schaick was seriously injured while fighting an enemy armed with a bolo during the encounter.

In 1906, he met Nellie Kellogg (from the Kellogg cereal family), an American school teacher working in the Philippines. They married and had one son, John, who died before his first birthday while the family was transporting him back to the US for medical care in 1907.

He served under GEN John Pershing in pursuit of Pancho Villa in Mexico and again as part of the American Expeditionary Force in World War I. In 1922, he and Nellie adopted a baby girl who was the daughter of an Army private and a Russian-born mother who had died unexpectedly. Their adopted daughter, Mary, died from appendicitis in 1937.

COL Van Schaick retired in 1934 and made his home in Baguio (Philippines). When the Japanese captured the country during World War II, both he and his wife were sent to POW camps where they lived for more than three years. Just a few weeks after his release in February 1945, Van Schaick died of an unspecified illness. He was 69 years old.

MEDAL OF HONOR – OMAHA BEACH

1LT Jimmie W. Monteith, USA
June 6, 1944
Normandy American Cemetery

Jimmie Monteith was working for his father's coal company in Virginia when he was drafted into the Army in 1941. In March 1942, he earned a commission as a Second Lieutenant and fought in Sicily in 1943 as part of the 1st Infantry Division.

On D-Day, Monteith led L Company of the 16th Infantry Regiment, 1st Division ashore at Omaha Beach. He demonstrated great courage by crossing the beach several times under intense fire. While on foot, he personally directed two tanks across a minefield so they could provide critical support for the beleaguered landing team.

Returning to L Company, he was ordered by CAPT John Armellino to seize a German fortification point which held a commanding position atop the 130-foot cliffside. Despite daunting odds, L Company successfully penetrated the Cabourg Draw area—a section essential to allow American combat vehicles to exit the beach. His unit continued to attack, although a German counterattack several hours later managed to surround their unit. Monteith fought bravely, launching several grenades and personally inflicting extensive casualties, but was eventually killed by German fire from the rear. CAPT Armellino, upon learning of 1LT Monteith's death, nominated him for the Medal of Honor. He is one of three men awarded the Medal for their bravery on Omaha Beach.

JIMMIE W. MONTEITH JR
1 LT 16 INF 1 DIV
VIRGINIA JUNE 6 1944
MEDAL of HONOR

ERNEST W. PRUSSMAN
PFC 13 INF 8 DIV
MASSACHUSETTS SEPT 8 1944
MEDAL OF HONOR

MEDAL OF HONOR

PFC Ernest W. Prussman, USA
September 8, 1944
Brittany American Cemetery

Ernest Prussman survived nearly two years in the US Army. Ernest and his twin brother, Earl, were born in Baltimore, MD, although the family later moved to Brighton, MA. His parents, Herbert and Helen, had four sons. One brother, Henry, served as an officer in the Army Air Force and another, Calvin, was a Navy radioman. Before the war, Ernest worked at Devonshire Cafeteria in Brighton.

He entered the Army in October 1942 and landed on Utah Beach (Normandy) in July 1944 with the 13th Infantry Regiment, 8th Infantry Division. The unit moved to Brittany (France) in August, and, in just one day, liberated Rennes to cheering crowds. However, the 8th Infantry faced intense fighting over the next several months.

On September 8, two battalions of the 13th Infantry launched an attack to capture the town of Pontanezen (France). By evening both battalions of the 13th Infantry had achieved their objectives, but Ernest Prussman never realized their success. He posthumously received the Medal of Honor for leading a squad against enemy mortars, machine guns, and snipers. Prussman destroyed one machine gun position and moved ahead of his colleagues to attack another. He was mortally wounded by an enemy rifleman, but as he fell, he threw a hand grenade and killed his attacker. Ernest Prussman died one week after his 23rd birthday.

TWO MEDALS OF HONOR

SGT Matej Kocak, USMC
October 4, 1918
Meuse-Argonne American Cemetery

Nineteen men have received two Medals of Honor. Five men—all from World War I—received the honor for the same act of valor, including Matej Kocak, who received both the Army and Navy Medals of Honor.

Matej Kocak was born in the Kingdom of Hungary in 1882 and immigrated to the US in 1906. The following year, he enlisted in the United States Marine Corps. He is one of eight Marines to be awarded the Medal of Honor in World War I.

During his third enlistment, he was assigned to the 66th Company, 5th Regiment and arrived in Saint-Nazaire, France, on December 31, 1917. He single-handedly stormed a machine-gun nest and then hours later led 25 French colonial soldiers to attack another nest during the attack at Villers Cotteret Wood (south of Soissons, France). He was killed in the same region just three months after his heroic acts on October 4th, during the Battle of Blanc Mont Ridge (part of the Meuse-Argonne Offensive). A ship in the Navy Sealift Command was named for Matej Kocak; it was removed from service in March 2023.

127

FREDDIE STOWERS
CORPL. 371 INF. 93 DIV.
SOUTH CAROLINA SEPT. 28, 1918

M.H., U.S.A.

MEDA

"He was a nice boy, nice to his family and to his mother and father."
Georgina Palmer, sister

FIRST BLACK MEDAL OF HONOR

CPL Freddie Stowers, USA
September 28, 1918
Meuse-Argonne American Cemetery

Two of Freddie Stowers' sisters received his Medal of Honor at a White House ceremony in April 1991, nearly 73 years after he was nominated for the award by his commanding officer. He is the first Black soldier from World War I to receive the Medal of Honor.

Freddie was the grandson of a slave and the fourth of 12 children born to Wiley and Annie Stowers in Sandy Springs, SC. Before he was drafted into the Army in October 1917, he worked as a farmhand on an Anderson County vegetable farm. He shipped off to France in April 1918 as part of the all-Black 371st Infantry Regiment, 93rd Division.

On September 28, 1918, Company C began their attack on Hill 188 in the Champagne Marne Sector. Shortly after the offensive began, the enemy ceased firing, climbed out of their trenches, and indicated they were surrendering. As American forces advanced, the Germans jumped back into their trenches and annihilated the exposed men using machine gun and mortar fire. At least 40% of the 200 Black soldiers in Company C perished in the battle. Stowers' Medal of Honor citation states:

> "Displaying great courage and intrepidity, CPL Stowers continued to press the attack against a determined enemy. While crawling forward and urging his men to continue the attack on a second trench line, he was gravely wounded by machine-gun fire. Although CPL Stowers was mortally wounded, he pressed forward, urging on the members of his squad, until he died."

Freddie Stowers left behind a wife, Pearl, and his daughter, Minnie Lee. He was 22 years old.

PARATROOPER MEDAL OF HONOR

PVT George Peters, USA
March 24, 1945
Netherlands American Cemetery

George Peters was the youngest son and one of seven children born to José and Angelina Peters who immigrated to the US from Portugal. He entered the Army in 1943 from Cranston, RI and joined the paratroopers. His niece, Debra Faviccio, said, "(H)e was afraid of heights. Yet...he decided to be a paratrooper, and it was simply because they received more money. He knew that would mean he could send more home...." George was a radio operator for G company, 3rd Battalion, 507th Parachute Infantry Regiment. On March 24, 1945, Peters was dropped near the Rhine River in northwestern Germany during Operation Varsity, which involved more than 16,000 Allied paratroopers. His unit of approximately 10 men landed in an open field near Flüren. Unfortunately, that placed them close to German machine-gun nests, and the paratroopers were pinned down before they could free themselves of their parachutes. Peters decided to launch his own one-man charge at the Nazis. His Medal of Honor citation notes:

> *"Once more he was torn by bullets, and this time he was unable to rise. With gallant devotion to his self-imposed mission, he crawled directly into the fire that had mortally wounded him until close enough to hurl grenades which knocked out the machine gun, killed two of its operators, and drove protecting riflemen from their positions into the safety of a woods. By his intrepidity and supreme sacrifice, PVT Peters saved the lives of many of his fellow soldiers."*

Years later, Joan Parenteau said of her uncle: "He was very close to my mom...[She] always said he was a protector. He was always selfless, and I think that really speaks to what he did." George Peters died six days after his 21st birthday.

GEORGE J. PETERS
PVT 507 PRCHT INF REGT
RHODE ISLAND MAR 24 1945
MEDAL of HONOR

ROBERT G. COLE
LT COL 502 PRCHT INF 101 ABN DIV
TEXAS SEPT 18 1944
MEDAL of HONOR

MEDAL OF HONOR – ARMY LT COLONEL

LTC Robert Cole, USA
September 18, 1944
Netherlands American Cemetery

Nicknamed "Coley" while playing B-squad football at the United States Military Academy at West Point, Robert Cole earned his commission in 1939. Hailing from San Antonio, TX, Cole was the son of an Army doctor, COL Clarence Cole, and his wife, Clara. On June 12, 1940, he returned home to marry his long-time sweetheart, Allie Mae Wilson, and they had one son, Robert Bruce Cole. In 1941, the young officer earned his jump wings and joined the 101st Airborne. He is reported to have been the first man to jump from the lead aircraft just after midnight on D-Day, June 6, 1944, in the skies over Normandy.

In the days following the Normandy landing, the 502nd Parachute Infantry Regiment (PIR) was tasked with taking the town of Carentan so that the forces from Utah and Omaha Beaches could link up. In the battle to take four key bridges, Cole found his unit pinned down by heavy gunfire from well-defended German positions. After an hour of witnessing heavy casualties, Cole decided the only option was to move forward and ordered the men to "fix bayonets." Cole personally led the charge into Nazi gunfire. A German prisoner from the battle was quoted as saying, "They charged like wild animals, (and)...screamed and shouted when they charged into our fire. It was unbelievable." Cole's men secured the bridgehead over the Douve River, suffering roughly a 50% casualty rate. His actions in Carentan would earn him the Medal of Honor.

Cole and the 3rd Battalion of the 502nd PIR parachuted into the Netherlands on September 17, 1944, for Operation Market Garden. He was killed by an enemy sniper the next day while signaling American P-47 aircraft. On October 30, 1944, his mother, Clara, received his Medal of Honor with Cole's wife and infant son in attendance. Robert Cole was 29 years old.

"One of our ablest and certainly one of our most gallant officers."

GEN Dwight Eisenhower in a note of condolence to Robert Cole's wife.

POET, FATHER AND INFANTRYMAN

SGT Joyce Kilmer, USA
July 30, 1918
Oise-Aisne American Cemetery

Joyce Kilmer's life was unfolding rather nicely. A graduate of Columbia University, he was married with children, had published four books, and was working for the *New York Times*. In 1913, he published his poem "Trees," for which he is best known. Although he was exempt from service due to his marital status, Mr. Kilmer decided to enlist in 1917. Arriving in France, he was initially assigned to the Regimental Chaplain as a statistician, but soon requested a transfer to the infantry. As part of the 165th Infantry Regiment, he was involved in many reconnaissance missions, but was killed by a German sniper during the Second Battle of the Marne (1918). SGT Kilmer was posthumously awarded the French Croix de Guerre for bravery. His comrade, SGT MAJ Ester, said:

> "[Kilmer] would always be doing more than his orders…getting nearer to the enemy positions than any officer would be inclined to send him."

Kilmer was survived by his wife, Aline, and four children. He was 31 years old.

JOYCE KILMER
SERGT. 165 INF. 42 DIV.
NEW YORK JULY 30, 1918

KURT GRUBER
OFFICE OF STRATEGIC SERVICES
GERMANY MAR 20 1945

CIVILIAN SPY

Kurt Gruber, OSS
March 20, 1945
Ardennes American Cemetery

A native of Westphalia, Kurt Gruber and his brother, Karl, were members of the communist party in Germany (the KPD), pressing for coal miners' rights in the 1920s. By 1930, the Nazi party had become the second largest party in Germany. In 1931, a meeting between the fascist right and the communist left turned violent and Karl was shot and killed. Kurt stiffened his resistance, until one day in 1935 he got off a train in Berlin only to see his photograph on posters identifying him as a wanted man. Seeing Gestapo agents at the exits, he fled on foot and hopped on a departing tram just before the Gestapo reached him. With the KPD's help, he escaped to Prague where he lived until Czechoslovakia fell to the Nazis in 1939. Gruber escaped to Glasgow, where he married a local woman, Jessie Campbell Leith, and worked as a miner, joining the National Union of Scottish Mineworkers. The couple moved to London, where Gruber was recruited by the Office of Strategic Services (the OSS, the CIA's predecessor) in 1944.

On March 19, 1945, Gruber boarded a plane on a secret mission, code-named CHISEL. His objective was to parachute into Germany, east of the Rhine River. However, the plane crashed, killing all on board. Mr. Gruber carried no papers nor personal identification. Until the war ended, his widow was given little information on his whereabouts, which caused her to fall into a deep depression and miscarry their baby. In 1946, Gruber's wife was escorted blindfolded to an unnamed location where she was presented his Medal of Freedom, along with a citation lauding his bravery.

CIVILIAN SPY

CAPT Roderick Stephen G. Hall, OSS
February 20, 1945
Florence American Cemetery

As a young Army Lieutenant, Stephen Hall was convinced that the Nazis could be defeated in Italy if the Allies could destroy the Brenner Pass, the critical cut through the Italian Alps for troops and supplies. He was so certain that he wrote a letter to a deputy of the newly formed OSS (the precursor to the CIA) in 1943 outlining his daring plan to sabotage the Brenner Pass and volunteering himself for the job. By August 1944, he found himself alone in Nazi-controlled northern Italy. There he recruited partisans and led them on numerous sabotage missions, destroying enemy facilities, infrastructure, and communication lines. In a blinding snowstorm in January 1945, he was incapacitated by frostbite while traveling on skis to a sabotage mission. While being cared for by a local priest, he was betrayed by a local and was tortured by the SS for two weeks before being hanged. In November 1944, he wrote his final letter to his dad:

> *"Maybe I can get out, if the Teutonic population gets too numerous. If not, I'll be saying goodbye and thanks for giving me life. I've made mistakes, and haven't got very far as standards usually go, but no one can say I haven't done a lot of things with life, or enjoyed it."*

RODERICK STEPHEN G. HALL
CAPT 2677 REGT OSS
CONNECTICUT FEB 20 1945

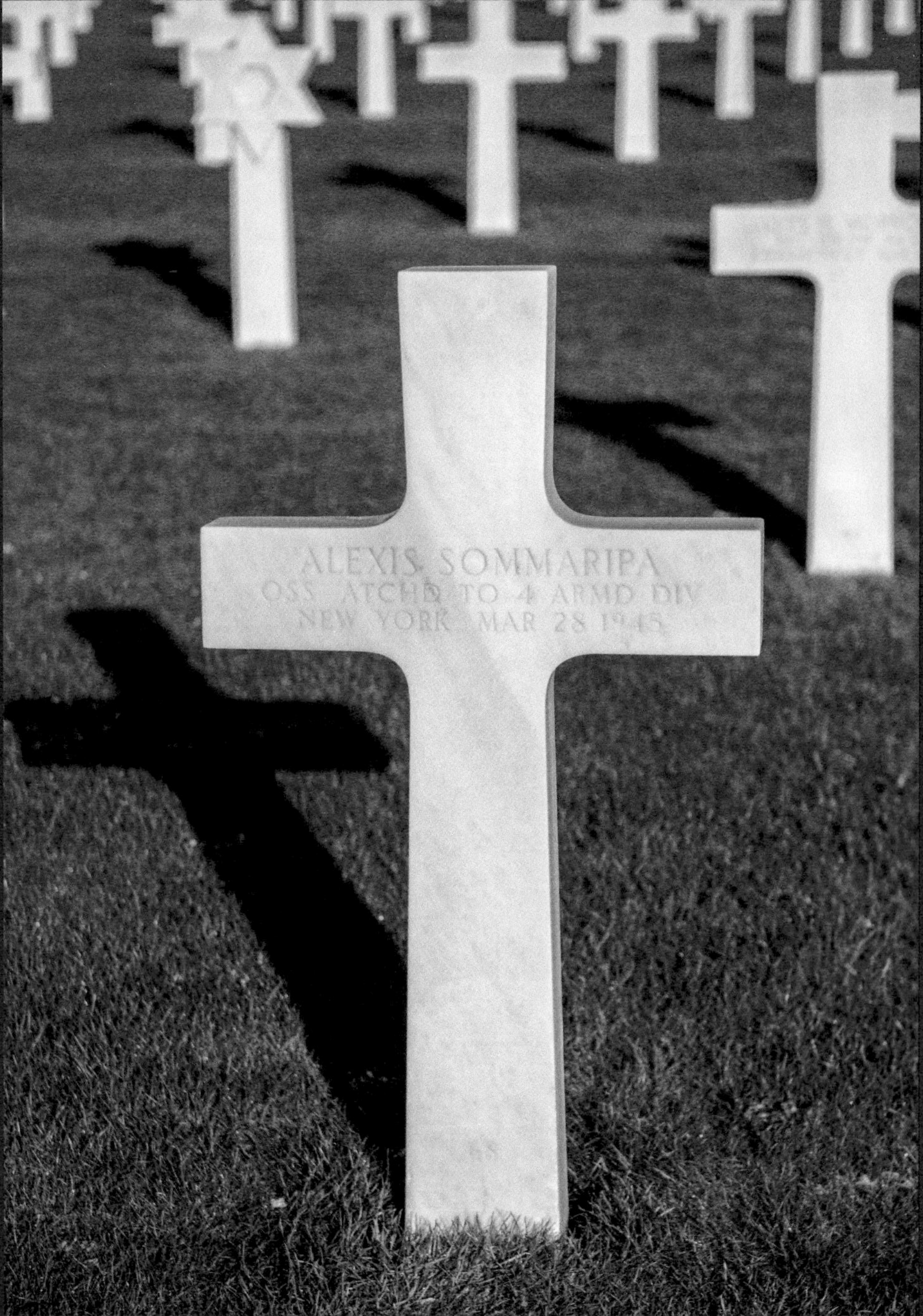
ALEXIS SOMMARIPA
OSS ATCHD TO 4 ARMD DIV
NEW YORK MAR 28 1945

CIVILIAN SPY

Alexis Ureyvitch Sommaripa, OSS
March 28, 1945
Luxembourg American Cemetery

Alexis Sommaripa was born in Odessa (then Russia) in 1900 to a wealthy family. He had two older brothers. His parents divorced in 1907, and his father, a respected judge in St. Petersburg, was sent to Siberia in 1916 for criticizing the Tsar's government.

After Alexis graduated from the Imperial Law School in Petrograd in 1918, he fled to America to escape the collapsed Russian Empire and the Communist Revolution. He sold his brother's stamp collection to fund his escape to Boston where he married a local widow, Alice Winslow, who had three daughters. He attended Harvard University where he earned a business degree. After Harvard, Alexis worked for Dupont de Nemours, Inc., in the 1920s and 1930s where he was involved in creating new fabrics such as rayon. He spoke several languages including French, Russian, German, and English, and enlisted at the age of 41 as the US entered World War II. After additional training, he was sent to England as an OSS Civilian Technician in 1943.

He landed at Omaha Beach on June 9, 1944, where he gathered intelligence from French underground partisans, and was part of combat operations at Carentan and Mortain (France) later that summer. Known for his "Psych War" tank equipped with a loudspeaker, Alexis was the only civilian tank commander in the US Army. He encouraged enemy soldiers to surrender and is credited with having captured upwards of 8,000 Nazis without a shot being fired. His "PsyOps" efforts often exposed him to enemy fire, and he went behind enemy lines to negotiate surrender with Nazi officers. He died in Germany after his tank was strafed by aircraft fire and crashed into a bomb crater. He was thrown from the vehicle, then the tank rolled on top of him, crushing him to death. His then teenage son, Amory, received his military medals from the Army. Twenty years after his death, Amory received (from one of his father's lovers) two diaries that Alexis had kept since the age of eight.

MERCHANT MARINE FROM PUERTO RICO

Francisco Charon, Merchant Seaman
January 9, 1945
Cambridge American Cemetery

Francisco Charon was the middle child born to José and Melitona Charon in October 1909 in Añasco, Puerto Rico. He had three brothers and three sisters, and served as a seaman with the Merchant Marines during the war. In March 1937, he married Carmen Lopez in Mayaguez (PR) and they had one son, César, who was born in 1938.

Charon was assigned to the American steamship Oremar on November 13, 1944, in support of the war supply efforts. On January 8, 1945, the vessel was docked at Ellesmere Port in Cheshire, England. While returning to his ship around 10:30 PM, Charon fell into the icy water alongside a poorly lit pier and drowned. A local man, Gerald O'Reilly, jumped into the water to save him, but his efforts proved unsuccessful. The official report estimates his time of death around 12:45 AM on January 9, 1945. Franciso Charon was 35 years old.

142

FRANCISCO CHARON
MERCHANT SEAMAN USMM
PUERTO RICO JAN 9 1945

NELSON R. BOWERS
PVT. 150 M. G. BATT'N. 42 DIV.
PENNSYLVANIA   JULY 24. 1918

LOST BROTHER

PVT Nelson Bowers, USA
July 24, 1918
Aisne-Marne American Cemetery

Nelson Bowers was born near Reading, PA, the youngest of three sons born to Wilson and Mamie Bowers. His father and his older brother, Robert, worked at a local rolling mill, while his oldest brother, Floyd, served as a Corporal with the 42nd Infantry Division. Floyd had one son, John, and was killed in action on July 28, 1918, in the Aisne-Marne counteroffensive.

Nelson enlisted in June 1917 and left for Europe aboard the SS Cedric, which departed New York City on November 14, 1917. He was attached to the 150th Machine Gun Battalion, 42nd Infantry Division, the same unit as his brother, Floyd. They fought at Chateau Thierry (France). Nelson drowned in the Marne River on July 24, 1918, just four days before Floyd was killed in action in the Aisne-Marne counteroffensive.

Their mother, Mamie, was divorced from her husband when her sons died in 1918. She learned of Floyd's death before Nelson's, but finally received a telegram from the Army on New Year's Day 1919 notifying her of Nelson's passing. Floyd is buried at Oise-Aisne American Cemetery, while Nelson is interred about a half-hour drive southwest at Aisne-Marne American Cemetery.

Robert, the surviving brother, had a son in 1920 whom he named after his brother, Nelson.

NATIVE AMERICAN

SGT Joe Little Squirrel, USA
August 28, 1944
Brittany American Cemetery

One of eight children born to Isaac and Ela Charley Squirrel, Joe Little Squirrel and at least one of his brothers, Lemuel C., enlisted in the Army. His family described Joe as an easy-going kid who spent time taking care of his father.

Joe was a Navajo who entered the service from his home state of Oklahoma and later received the Purple Heart Medal. He died in the Battle for Brest (France) as a soldier in the 9th Infantry Regiment, 2nd Division at the age of 22.

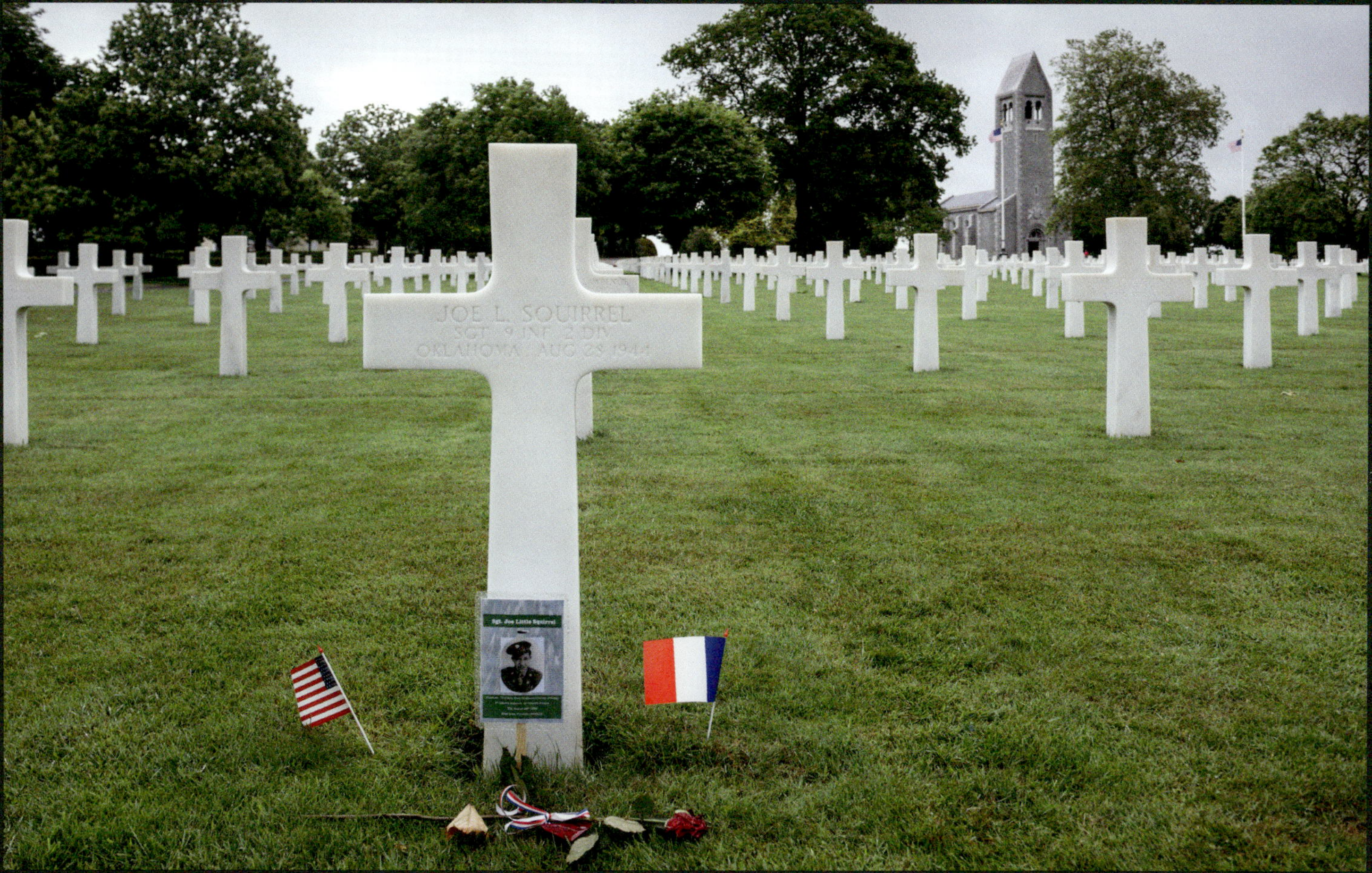
JOE L. SQUIRREL
SGT 9 INF 2 DIV
Sgt. Joe Little Squirrel

HENRY H. BOGER
2 LIEUT. 365 INF. 92 DIV.
ILLINOIS NOV. 11, 1918
AGE: 31
DEATH: KIA
SCHOOL: Univ of Illinois/Ohio State Univ/
Univ of Wisc
OCCUPATION: Chemistry instructor at
Tuskegee Institute
25

BLACK PROFESSOR

2LT Henry Hall Boger, USA
November 11, 1918
St. Mihiel American Cemetery

Henry (Hank) Hall Boger was killed in action in the Argonne Forest (France) on November 11, 1918, the same day the Armistice was signed ending World War I. He was born in September 1887, the middle child of seven born to Calvin and Amy Boger of Aurora, IL. His father and two older brothers worked as masons in Illinois.

Hank Boger graduated from Ohio State University in 1914, where he was a member of the Agriculture Club and Alpha Phi Alpha fraternity. He taught in the Agricultural Department at Tuskegee Institute (now University) before the Great War. In June 1917, Boger enlisted in the Army and trained at Camp Dodge (Des Moines, IA) before sailing for Europe from Hoboken, NJ the following June aboard the steamship Agamemnon.

He served with the all-Black 92nd Infantry Division ("Buffalo Soldiers"), which was the only Black unit that saw combat in World War I, specifically during the Meuse-Argonne Offensive. Just 11 days after Boger was killed, his mother, Amy, passed away. Hank Boger was 31 years old.

CHOCTAW CODE TALKER

PVT Andrew Perry, USA
August 20, 1944
Rhone American Cemetery

Andrew Perry was part of the proud contingent of Choctaw Code Talkers whose service dates back to World War I, six years before Native Americans were officially considered American citizens. In both world wars, the US Army relied on Native Americans to use their native languages—many never written down and therefore considered unbreakable by enemy forces—as a code to transmit critical battlefront communications among combat units.

Perry was born in November 1920 to Louis and Susanna Perry in Oklahoma. He grew up with four sisters, a brother, Leo, with whom he was very close, and a half-brother. He enlisted in September 1940 and served as a Code Talker with the 45th Infantry Division. Andrew Perry participated in the Allied landings in North Africa, then in Sicily, then again in Italy, and finally on D-Day in Normandy. Perry died with four others while fighting a German tank division near Sainte Maxime (Mediterranean coast of France) just two months after the D-Day landings.

151

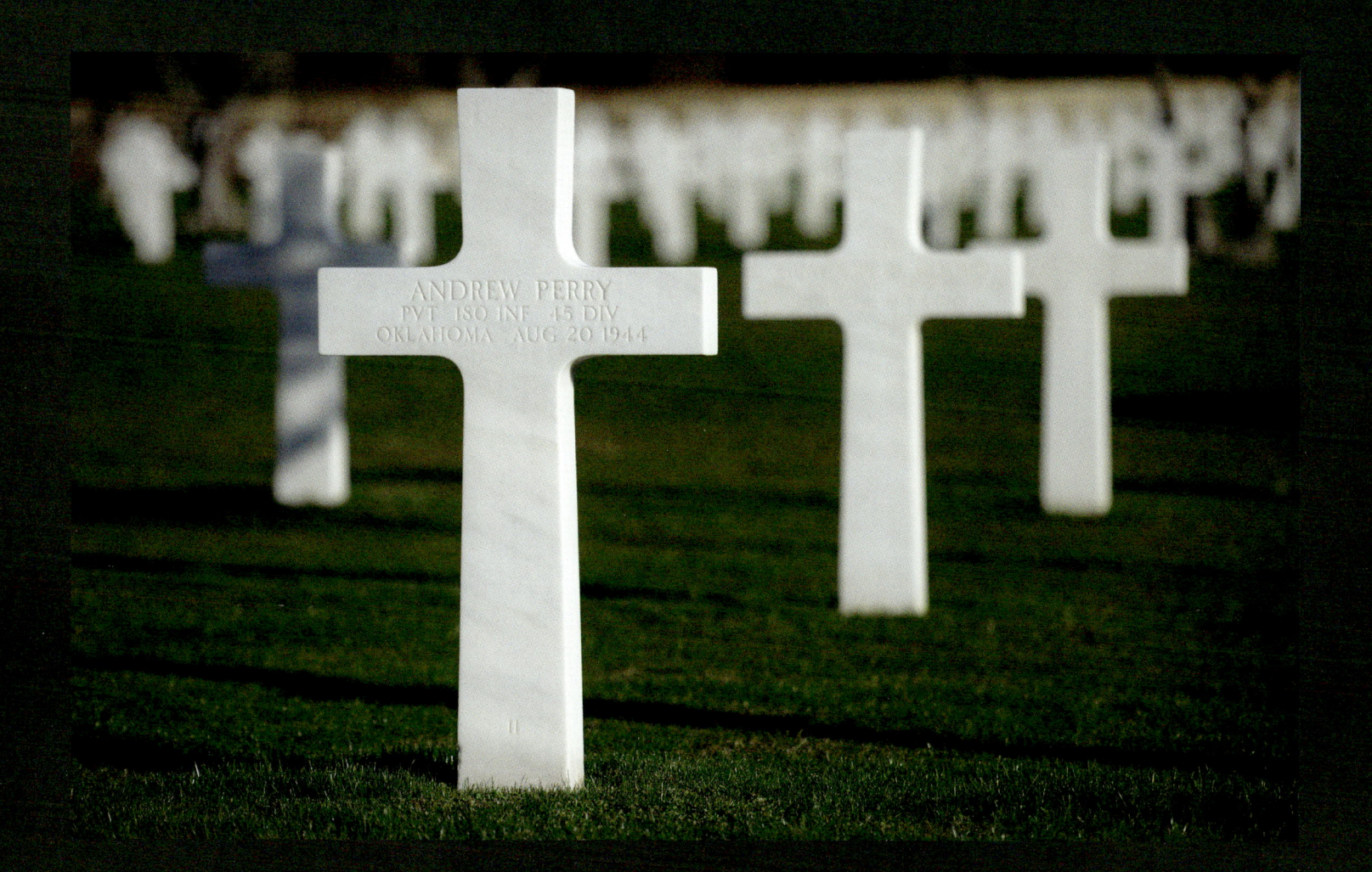

CARLIE DIAL
S SGT 831 BOMB SQ 485 BOMB GP (H)
NORTH CAROLINA   AUG 7 1944

"We said, Dear Dad and Mother, We will always be, The true and brave boys you taught us to be. When we are in a distant land, We want you dear ones to know, We are doing the best we can."

Poem written to hometown newspaper by PFC Carlie Dial in 1943

NATIVE AMERICAN TAIL GUNNER

SSGT Carlie Dial, USAAF
August 7, 1944
Ardennes American Cemetery

Carlie Dial entered the US Army Air Force in April 1943. He flew more than 35 combat missions as a B-24 tail gunner, including attacks on Munich (Germany), Trieste (Italy), and various targets in Hungary, Romania, Yugoslavia, and Austria through the summer of 1944.

Carlie's parents, Plummer and Dolly Dial, were Lumbees (often grouped with Cherokees). Carlie had four living siblings (three sisters and a brother), as well as two infant siblings who were deceased. The family worked as tenant farmers on private land in Lumberton, NC.

After he earned his wings, Dial deployed to Europe in early 1944, and was attached to the 831st Bomber Squadron flying out of Venosa, Italy. On August 7, he was on board a B-24 Liberator en route to Blechhammer (Germany) to bomb an oil field when his plane was attacked by German fighters near Gyor, Hungary. From his position in the tail, Dial shot down two enemy planes and crippled a third before a fourth aircraft hit him directly with 20 mm rounds and ignited the plane's hydraulic fluid. Dial's last words were, "Lower the wheels, skipper."

Eight of the ten crew members parachuted out of the burning aircraft and survived as POWs in Germany until May 1945. Crew member reports indicate that the Germans told the American aviators that, when they found the B-24, the only trace of Dial was one hand blackened from the fire.

Shortly before his death, Dial had received the Air Medal for "meritorious service" as a tail gunner. SSGT Dial was an experienced and effective gunner even though he was just 20 years old when he was killed.

38-YEAR-OLD PRIVATE

PVT Leonard Hofstetter, USA
November 8, 1942
North Africa American Cemetery

Leonard Hofstetter was drafted into the Army at the age of 37. Prior to being drafted, he attended Trinity Lutheran School and operated a newsstand for years on Franklin St. in Peoria, IL.

In May 1942, he was sent to Fort Knox (KY) and then to Ireland to prepare for the Army's invasion of North Africa. During Operation Torch, the American invasion of Algeria, Hofstetter landed in Algeria with the 6th Infantry Regiment, 1st Armored Division. He was killed by an enemy sniper as he came ashore at Oran (Algeria) on November 8, 1942. His parents, August and Anna, had died in the early 1920s. He was survived by two sisters, Juanita and Margaret.

Leonard Hofstetter never married and was 38 years old when he was killed. Just three days after his death, the United States Congress lowered the upper age limit for the draft to 37 years. He was remembered for having never complained about being drafted at his age and for saying it was better that he be sent than a man with a wife and children.

PVT. LEONARD HOFFSTETTER

Pvt. Hofstetter Killed In Africa

Formerly Operated Newsstand Here

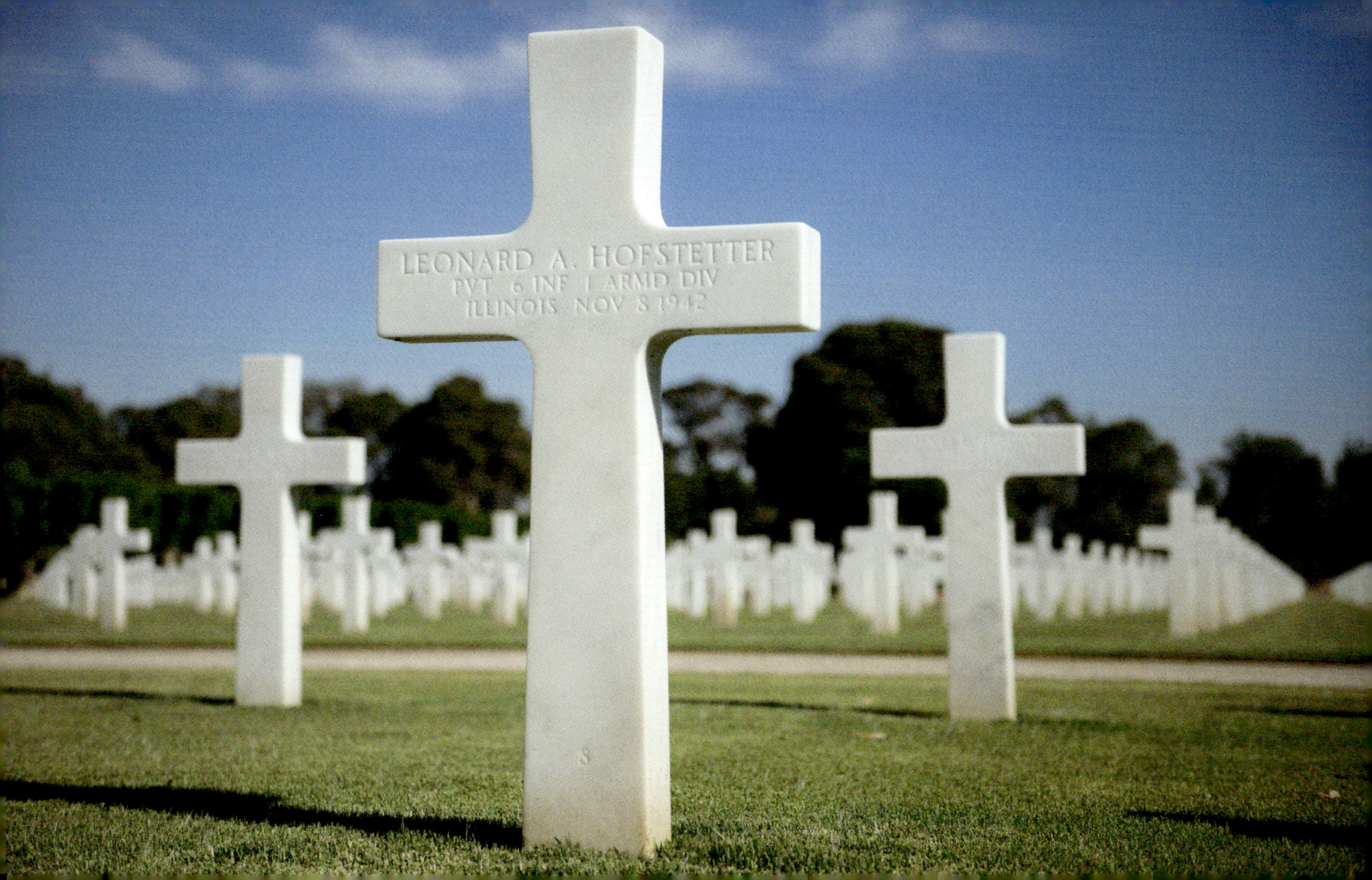
LEONARD A. HOFSTETTER
PVT 6 INF 1 ARMD DIV
ILLINOIS NOV 8 1942

MEUSE - ARGONNE

" I wish those people who write so glibly about this being a holy war and the orators who talk so much about going on, no matter how long the war lasts and what it may mean, could see a case of mustard gas—the poor things burnt and blistered all over with great mustard-coloured suppurating blisters, with blind eyes, all sticky and stuck together, and always fighting for breath, with voices a mere whisper, saying their throats are closing and they know they will choke."

BRITISH NURSE VERA BRITTAIN IN HER MEMOIR, *TESTAMENT OF YOUTH*

EPINAL

CHAPTER THREE | TAPS

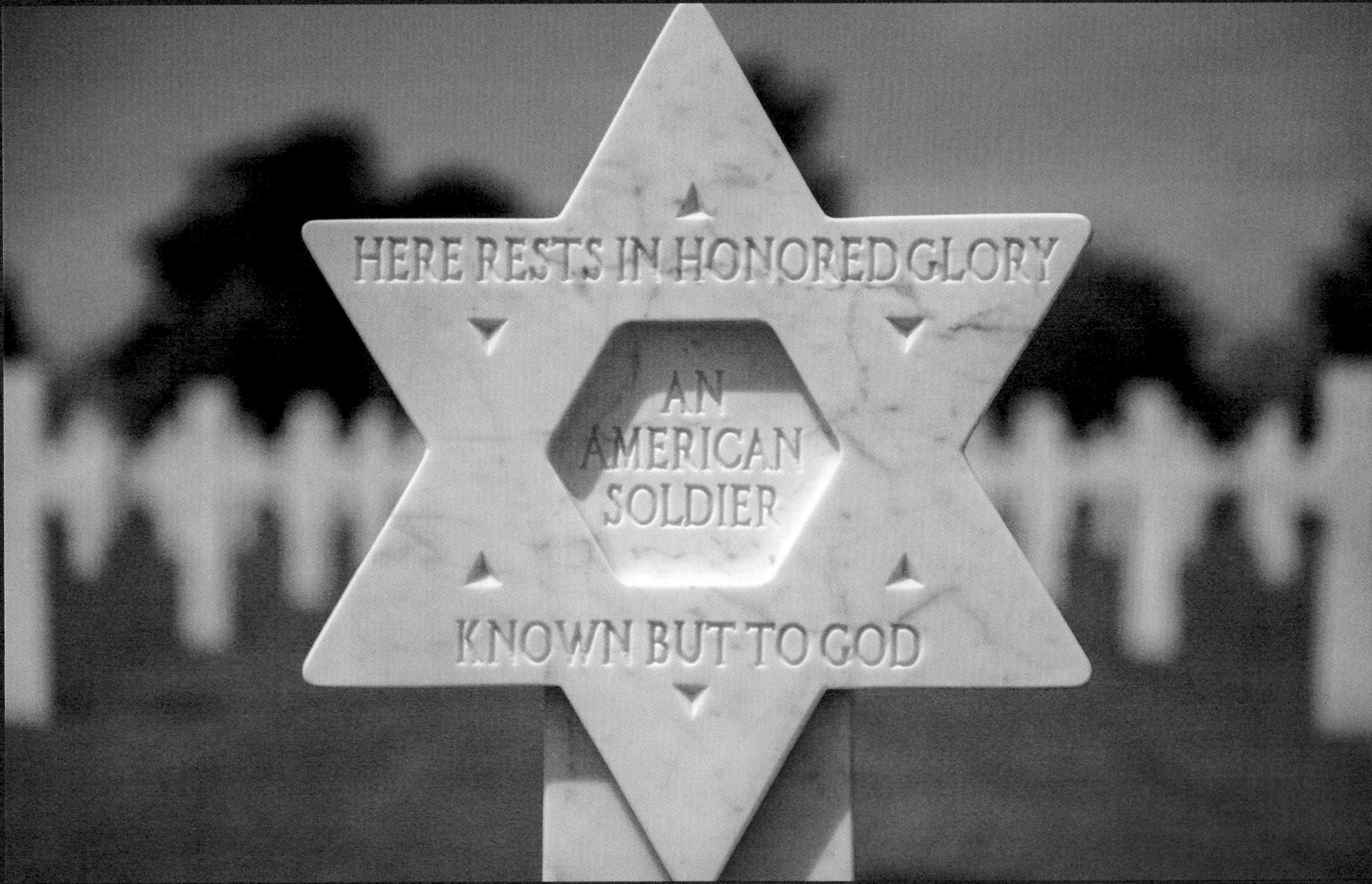
HERE RESTS IN HONORED GLORY
AN
AMERICAN
SOLDIER
KNOWN BUT TO GOD

ST. MIHIEL

IN HONORED MEMORY OF THOSE WHO GAVE THEIR LIVES FOR THEIR COUNTRY

HENRI - CHAPELLE

NETHERLANDS

NNES

CEVIL S. CONNER
PFC 11 INF 5 DIV
ARKANSAS JAN 23 1945

" WHAT I GAVE I HAVE "

AISNE - MARNE

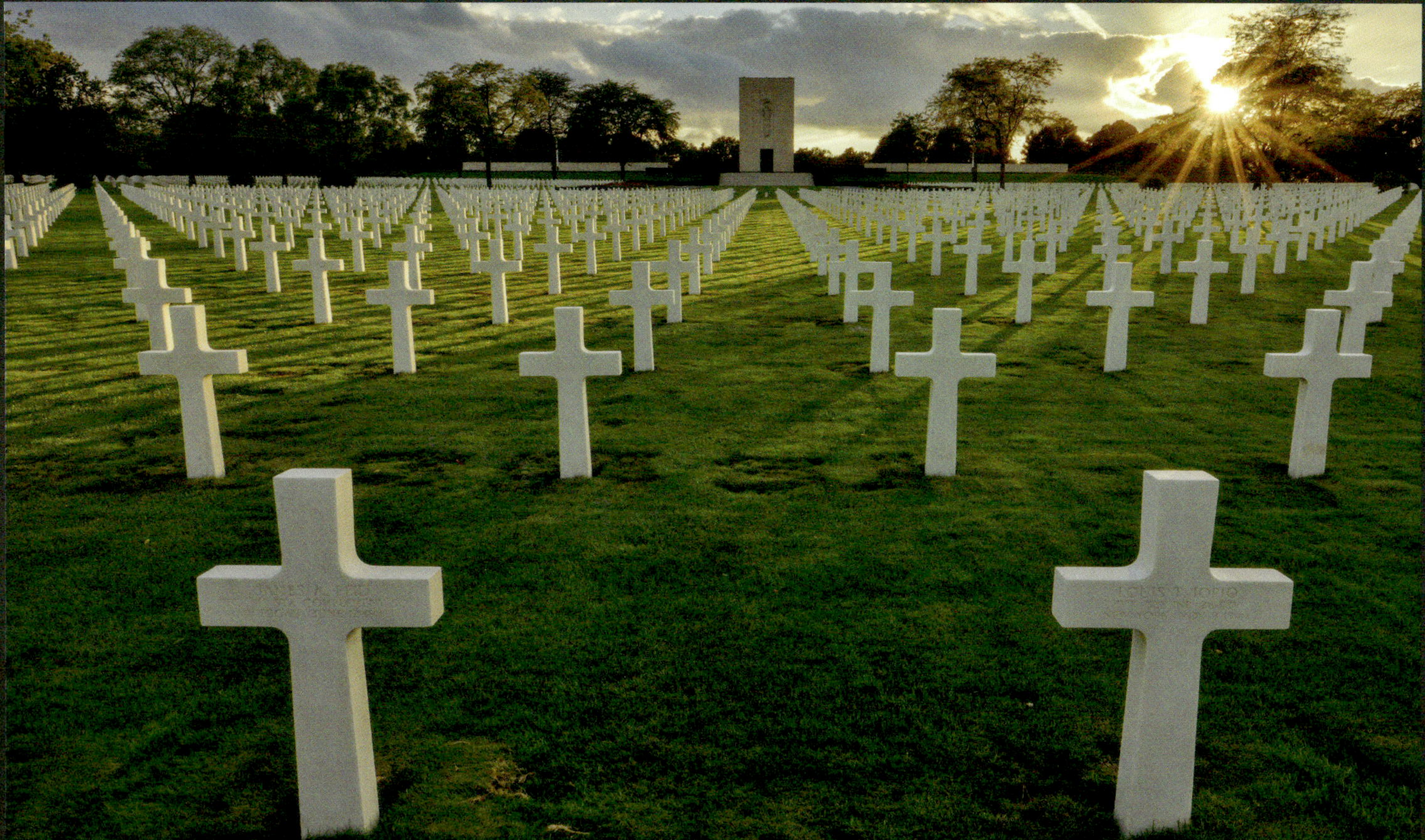

HENRI - CHAPELLE

SURESNES

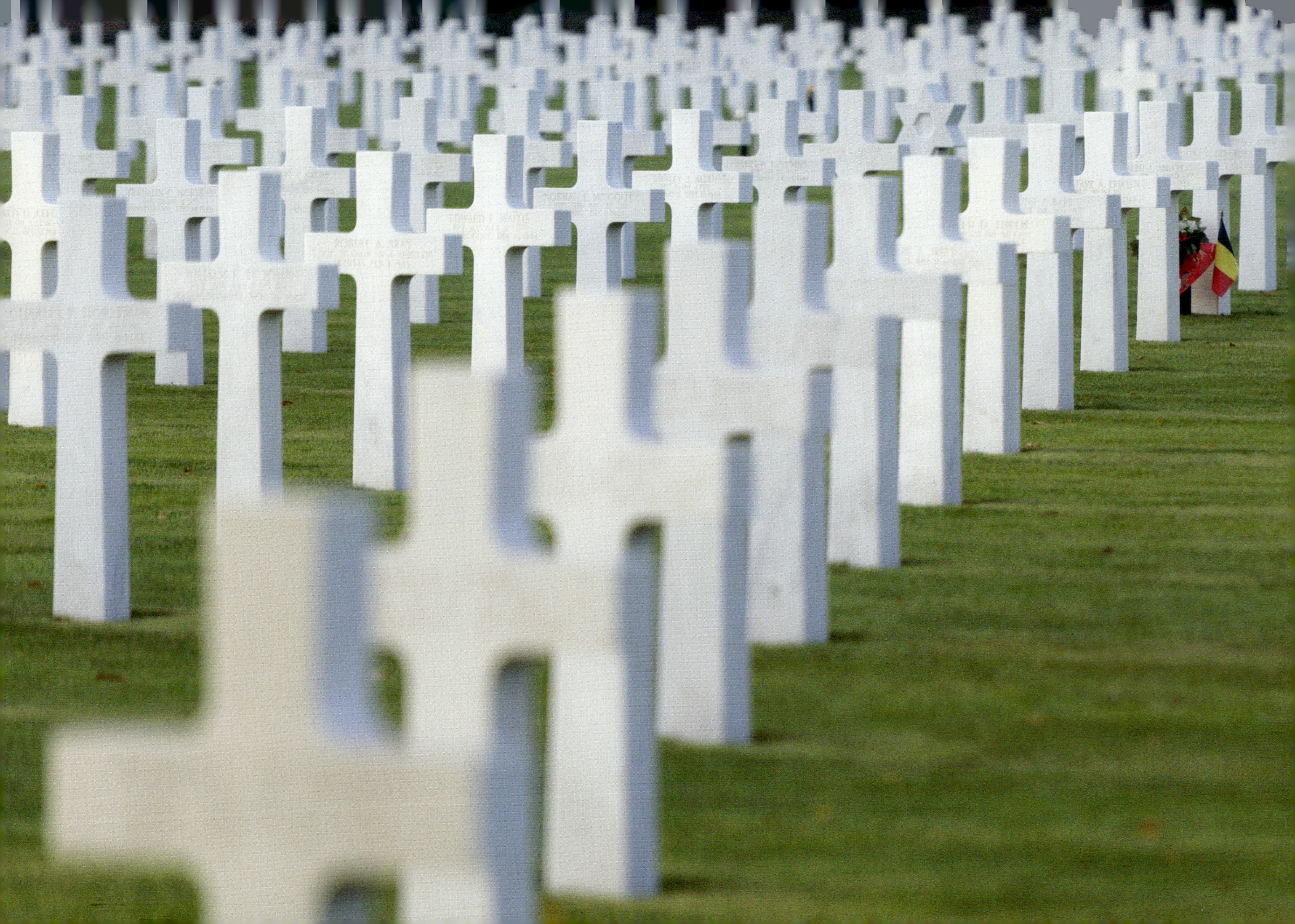

HENRI

	USN	NEW YORK
MATE 3C	USNR	R I
	USN	WEST VIRGINIA
	USNR	OKLAHOMA
T	USN	WYOMING
	USNR	KENTUCKY
	USNR	CONNECTICUT
	USNR	ALABAMA
ATE 2C	USN	KENTUCKY
	USNR	VIRGINIA
ENDER	USN	CALIFORNIA
	USN	TEXAS
3C	USNR	ILLINOIS
	USN	ILLINOIS
	USN	PHILIPPINES
	USNR	MICHIGAN
MAN 2C	USNR	ILLINOIS
	USN	MASSACHUSETTS
	USNR	MASSACHUSETTS
AN 2C	USN	COLORADO
GJ	USNR	TEXAS
S MATE	USN	NEW YORK
	USNR	MASSACHUSETTS
	USNR	MASSACHUSETTS
ATE 2C	USNR	NEW YORK
	USNR	OREGON
	USN	INDIANA
	USN	MICHIGAN
2C	USN	INDIANA
	USNR	ARKANSAS
	USNR	KANSAS
	USNR	NEW YORK
	USNR	PENNSYLVANIA
	USN	MISSOURI
	USNR	CALIFORNIA
IC	USNR	NEW JERSEY
G	USN	PENNSYLVANIA
	USNR	TEXAS
3C	USNR	PENNSYLVANIA
USNR		PENNSYLVANIA
3C	USNR	ILLINOIS
ATE IC	USNR	CALIFORNIA
	USNR	MASSACHUSETTS
	USNR	CONNECTICUT
	USN	PENNSYLVANIA

LEGGETT WOODR
LEGLER KENNETH
LEGROTTAGLIE JO
LEHARDY LOUIS
LEHMAN DONALD
LEHMICKE ALBERT
LEHNEN EDWARD
LEHNER WILLIAM
LEHNERTZ MARVIN
LEIBBRANDT CARL
LEICHT HOWARD
LEIGBER CARL L
LEIGH JUNIOR H
LEIGHT ANDREW
LEIGHTON JOHN
LEIMAN ELLIOTT
LEINTHAL DANIEL
LEIPPE DONALD
LEIR MAX C
LEISHMAN ROBERT
LEITZ DONALD
LEJEUNE PIERRE
LELAND LAWRENC
LELUIKA PAUL P
LEMACKS FRANCIS
LEMAY LEO O
LEMER LLO BENJA
LEMING WILLIAM
LEMKE PHILLIP A
LEMMON CHARLIE
LEMOURE EDWAR
LENDO JOHN
LENHART LESLIE
LENIG WALTER L
LENNARTZ CARL
LENTZI EUGENE
LENZ PAUL D
LEO NICHOLAS
LEOMBRONE JOSE
LEON NOLAN J
LEONARD CHARLE
LEONARD DANIE
LEONARD GRANT
LEONARD JAMES
LEONARD JOSEPH
LEONARD LELAN
LEONARD RALPH
LEONE SAMUEL J
LIONELLO CEASE

MANILA

LUXEMBOURG

RHONE

RHONE

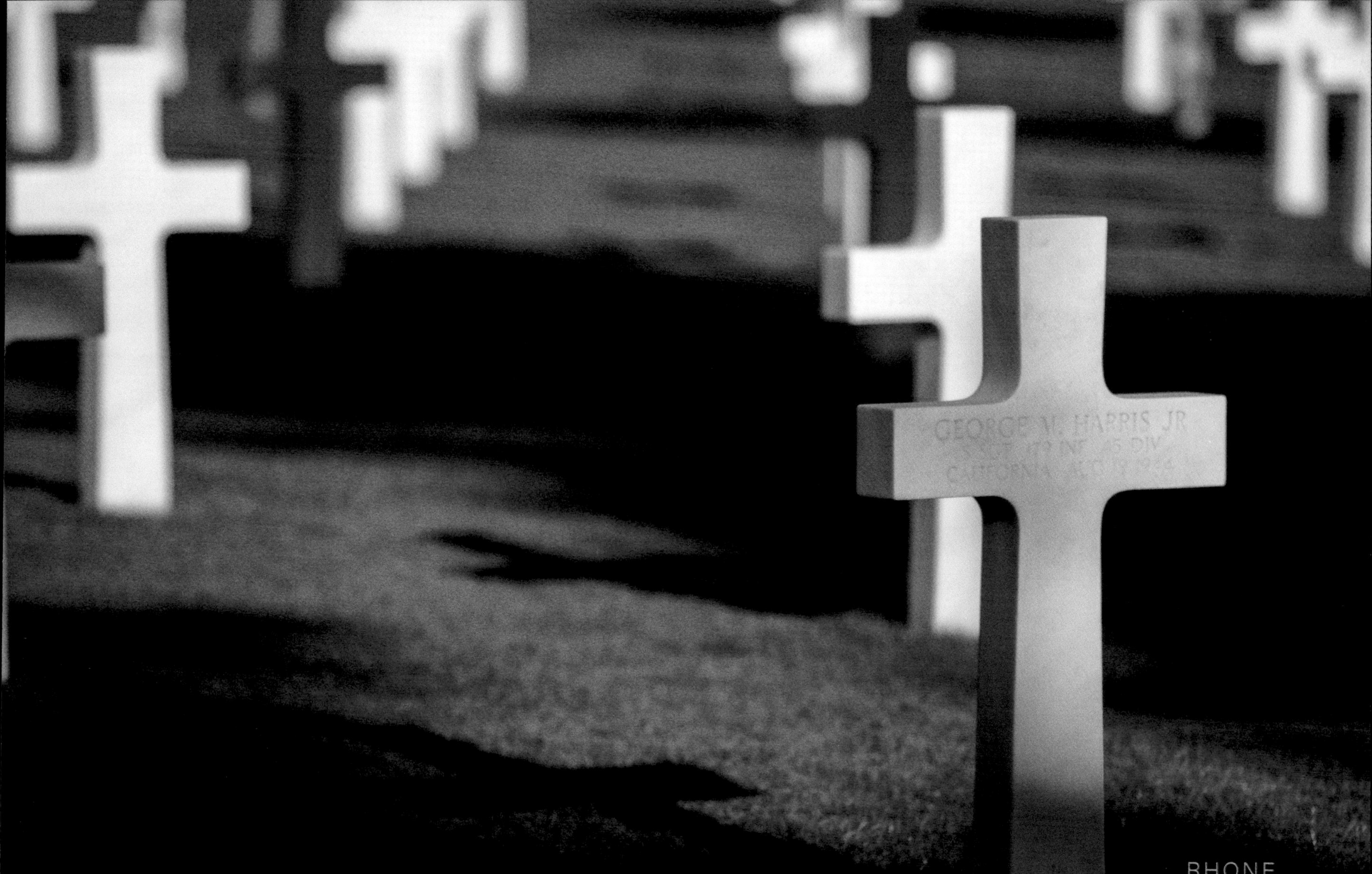

RHONE

RHONE

EPINAL

NAMES OF AMERICANS

NETHERLANDS

NETHERLANDS

FLANDERS FIELD

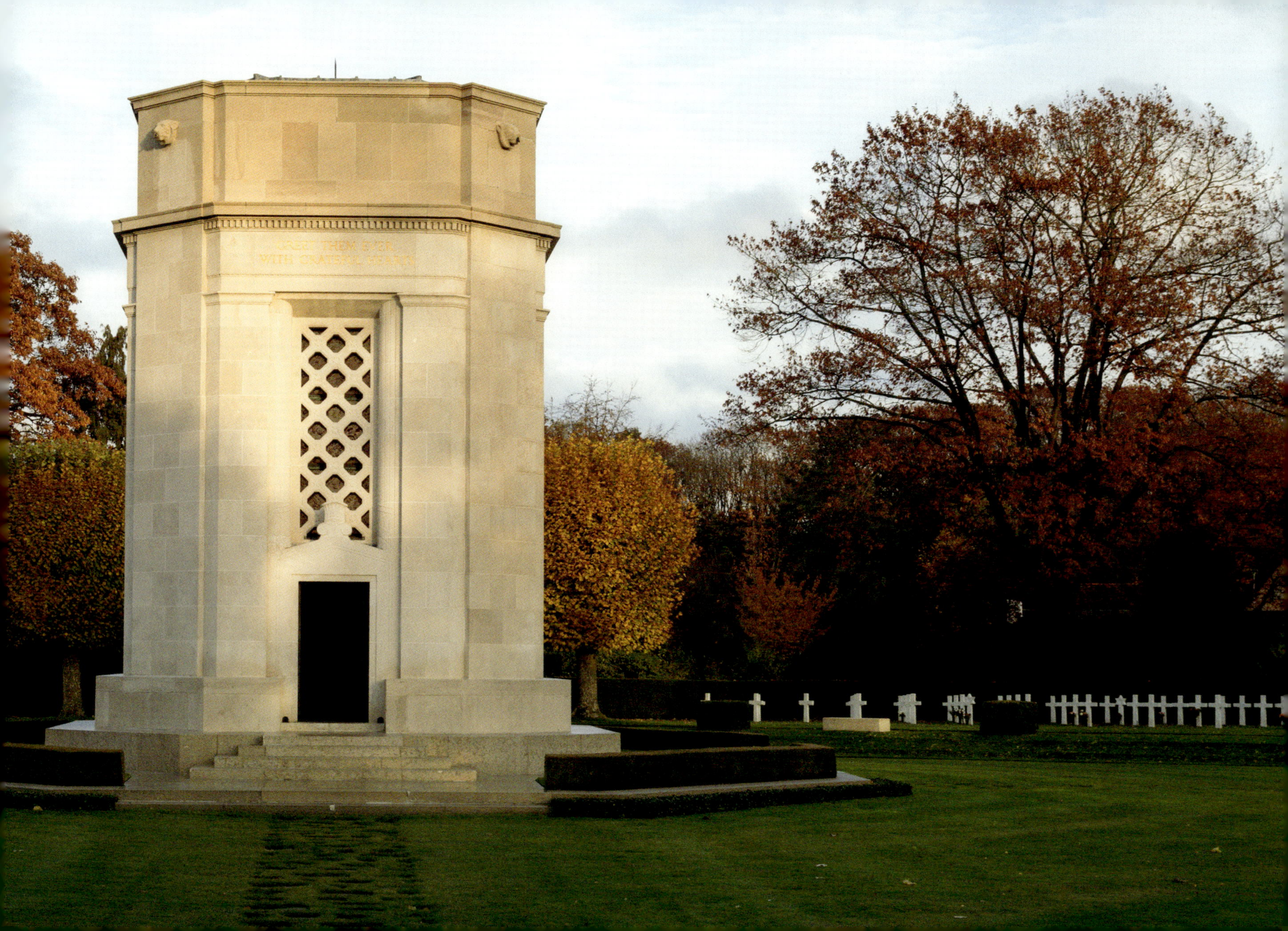
GREET THEM EVER
WITH GRATEFUL HEARTS

RHONE

LUXEMBOURG

RHONE

LUXEMBOURG

MEUSE - ARGONNE

MEUSE - ARGONNE

LUXEMBOURG

NETHERLANDS

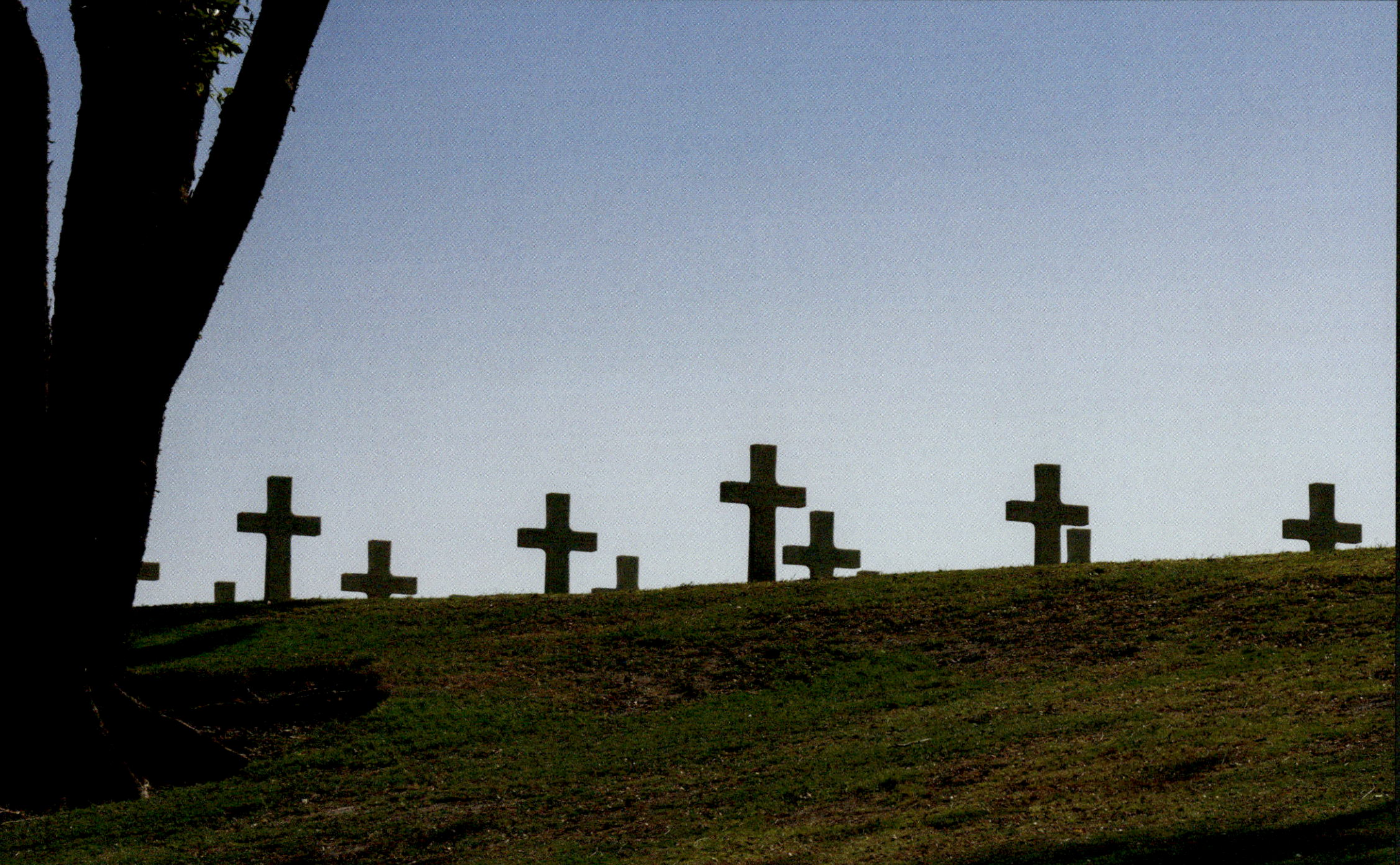

LORRAINE

MEUSE - ARGONNE

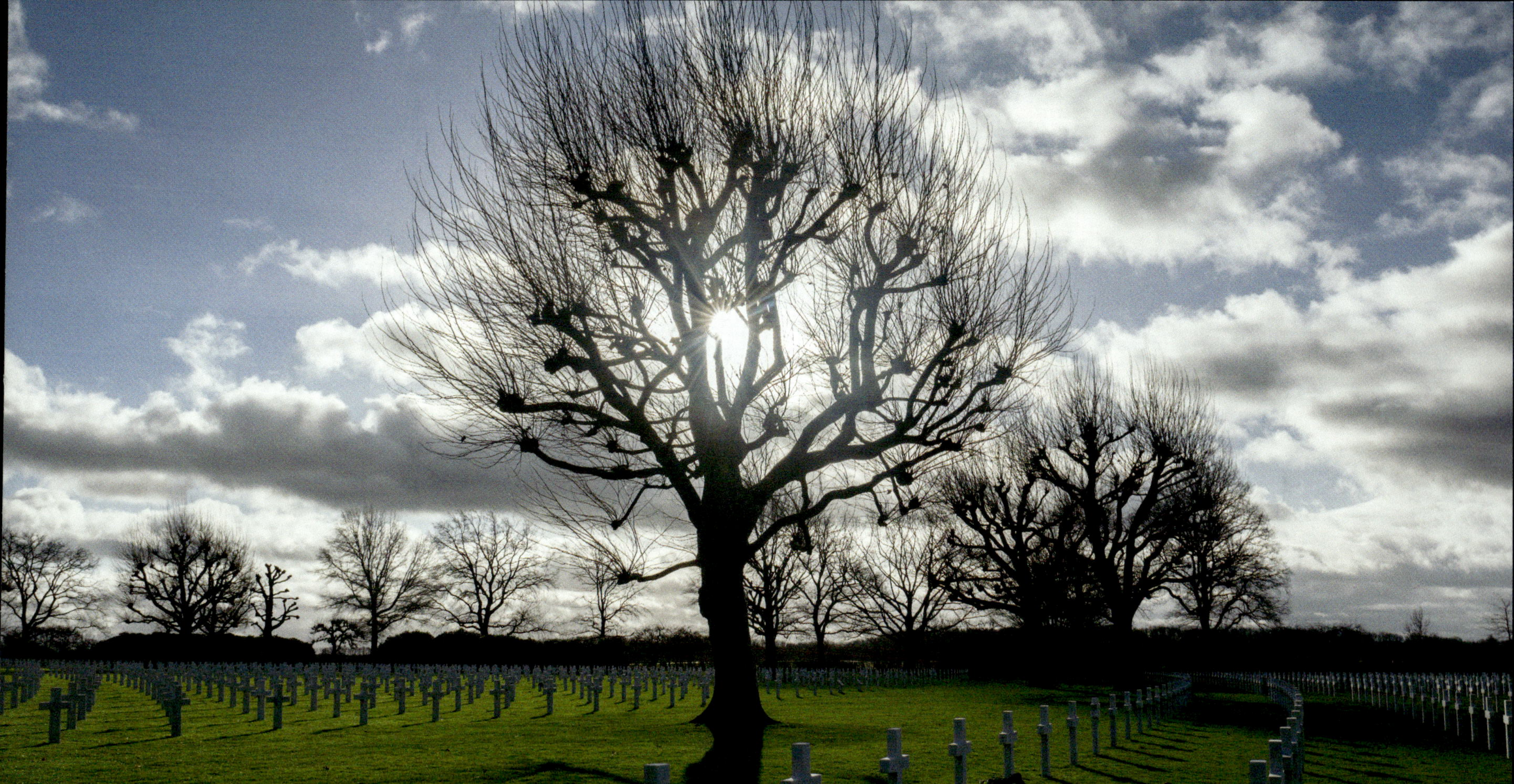

OISE - AISNE

MEUSE - ARGONNE

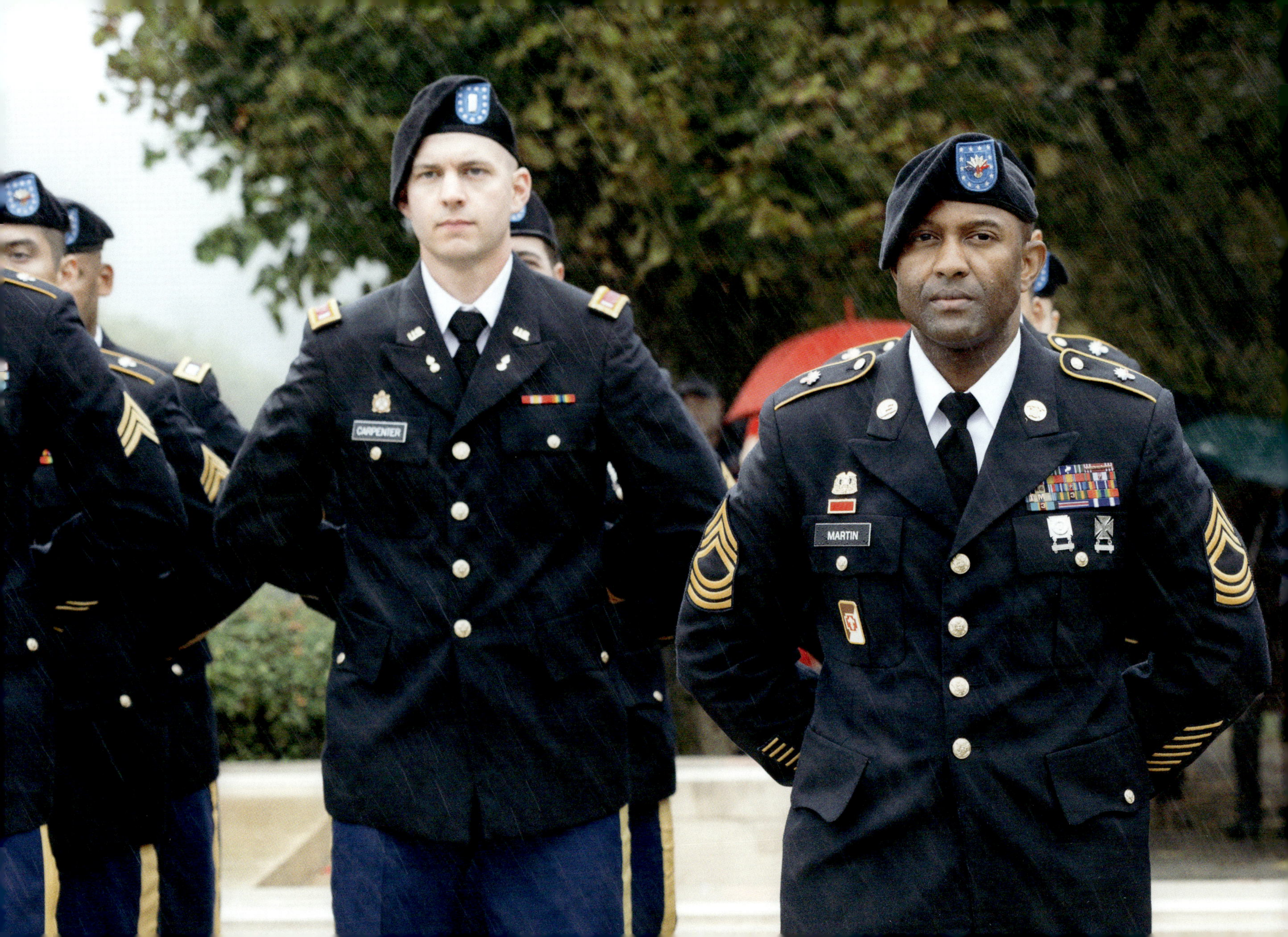
CARPENTER
MARTIN

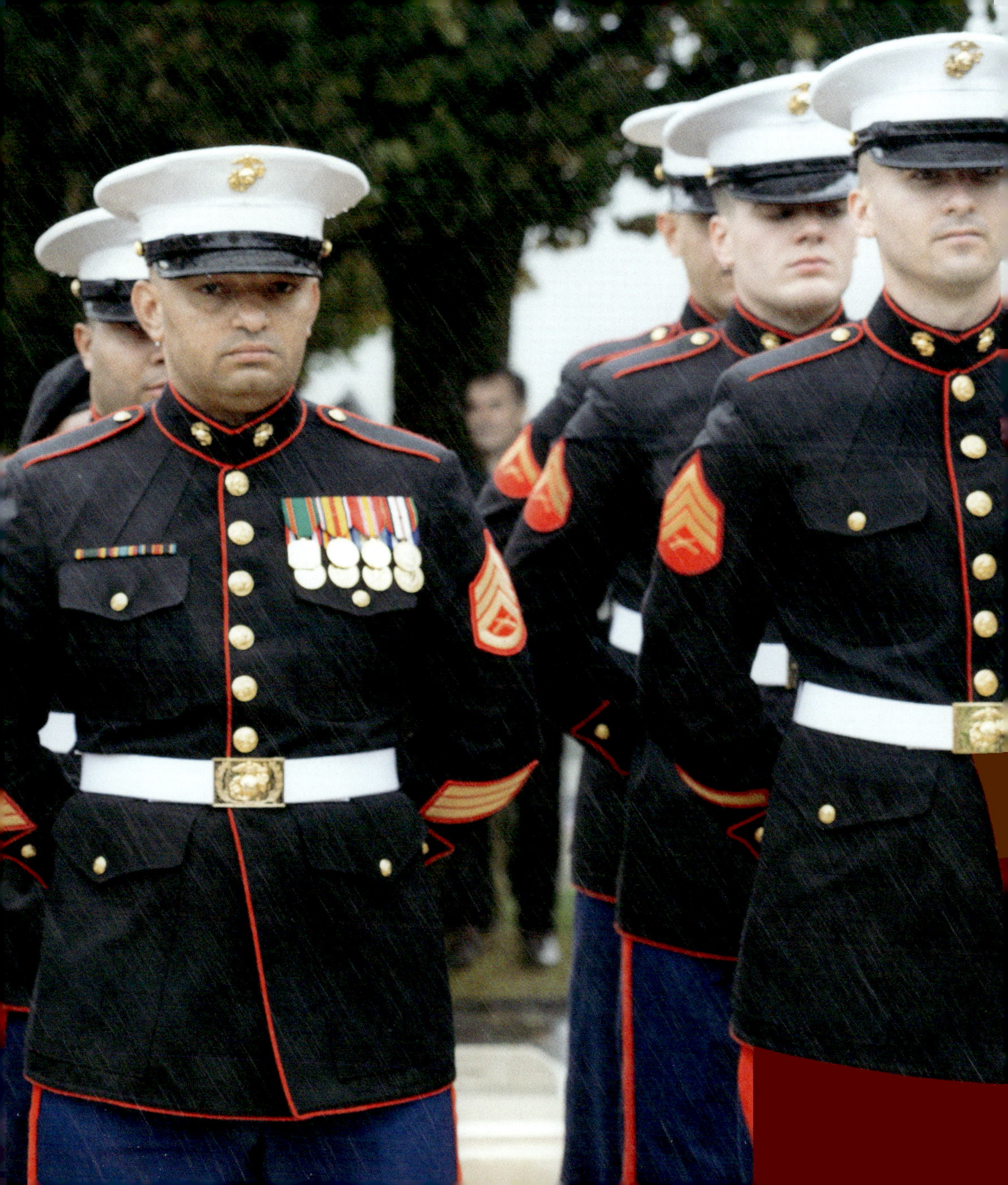

MEUSE - ARGONNE

NORMANDY

MEUSE - ARGONNE   MEUSE - ARGONNE

MEUSE - ARGONNE

ST. MIHIEL

NORMANDY

NORMANDY

EPINAL

LAFAYETTE ESCADRILLE

RMANDY

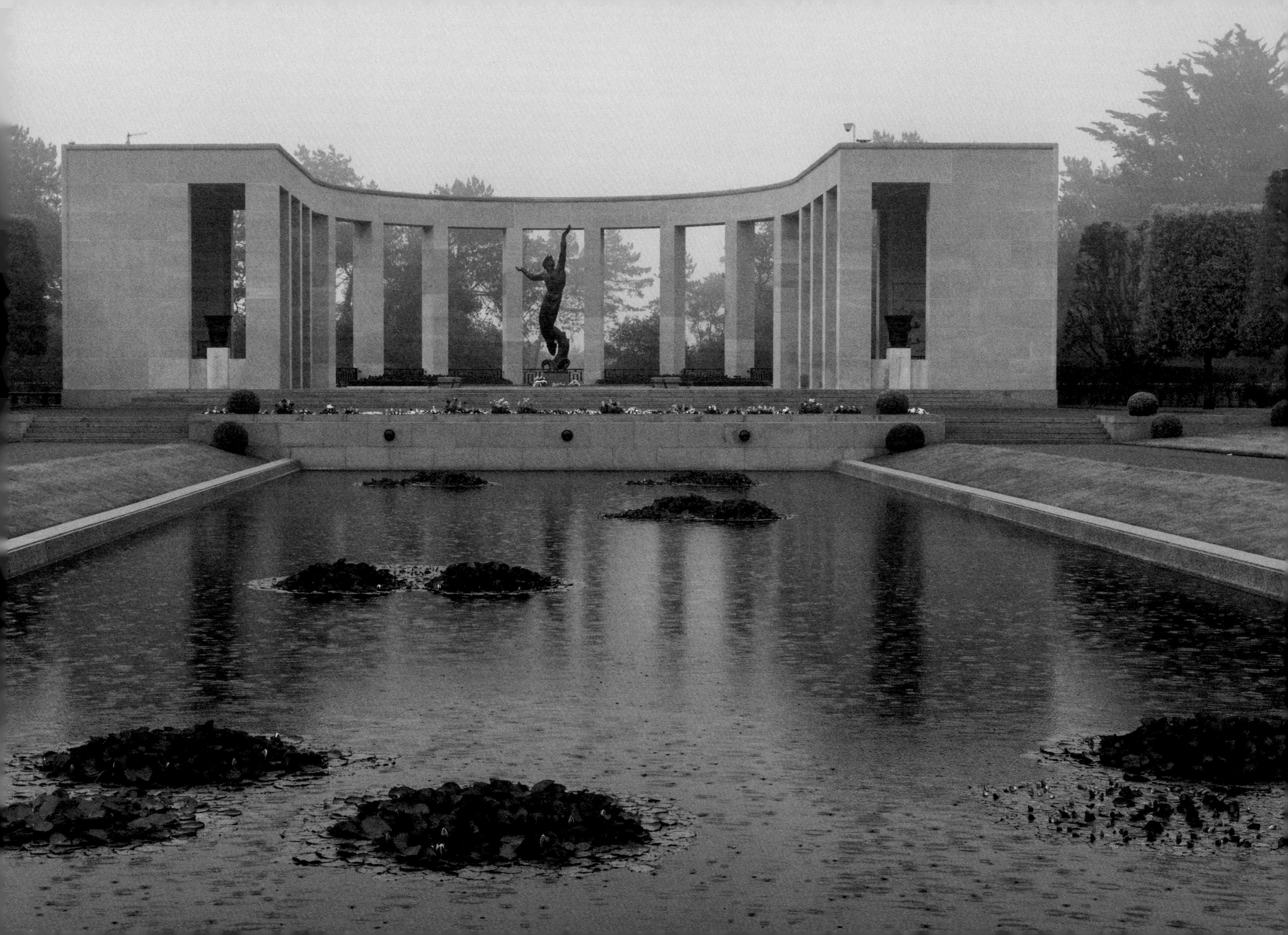

NORMANDY

NORMANDY

When World War I began, the United States had the 17th largest standing Army in the world with 127,500 men. The US Marine Corps was miniscule, with only 10,386 men, and the United States Air Force would not be established for another three decades.

GEN John Pershing was selected to lead the American Expeditionary Force (AEF) into World War I. He first set foot in England on June 8, 1917, but American troops would not begin combat operations until October 21, 1917, with the elite 1st Division of the US Army. However, broader deployment of American forces into combat occurred almost one year after Pershing's arrival in Europe in May 1918.

GEN Pershing is perhaps best known for two things as head of the AEF: despite vociferous demands from the Allies and some American politicians, he refused to place his inexperienced men into battle until they were fully trained—a process that, in most cases, took over a year. And, once in theatre, he insisted that American troops be commanded by American officers. In these actions, I believe GEN Pershing demonstrated his great respect for each man's life.

On March 4, 1923, President Warren Harding established the American Battle Monuments Commission (ABMC) to construct monuments that would honor the AEF. Then, in 1934, President Franklin Roosevelt expanded the ABMC's role, tasking it with also maintaining our overseas military cemeteries. It is therefore unsurprising that GEN John Pershing was selected to be the ABMC's first Chairman in 1923. He led the ABMC until his death in 1948.

I believe GEN Pershing's great respect for the lives of his troops helped to cement the American military's tenet: leave no one behind. For nearly a century now, the ABMC has meticulously maintained America's 26 overseas military cemeteries and 32 monuments, memorials, and markers around the world. The ABMC's hard work and commitment to its mission brings great honor to those interred and offers every person the opportunity to pay their respects to those who fought and died for freedom.

> *"The point I wish to make is that those things cause the soldier to remember that the people at home are behind him. You do not know how much that is going to mean to us who are going abroad. You do not know how much that means to any soldier who is over there carrying the flag for his country. That is the point which should be uppermost in the minds of those who are working for the soldier."*
>
> GEN John Pershing

BROOKWOOD
AMERICAN MILITARY
CEMETERY

Biography

As a photographer, I am aware of the lens through which I view life. From this perspective, I see the many blessings that God has bestowed on me: a wonderful wife, a great family, parents who sacrificed more than they could afford for my education, true friends, a pack of zany, funny, loving dogs. The list goes on; I am humbled by them. As a former Naval officer, the sacrifices made by military members and their families are never far from my mind. At this moment, many of our fellow Americans are in dangerous places where the only certainty is that you can rely on the soldiers, sailors, or Marines that are with you. To live in a society with freedom and justice is a great blessing, but those blessings come from the great sacrifices made by those who stepped into the breach when darkness, evil, and tyranny threatened all of us.

My father was a Korean War veteran (USS Ajax, AR-6); his older brother, Butch, was a Radioman in WWII (USS Sampson, DD 394); their cousin, Paul (Uncle Duke to me), served in the Air Force in the mid-1950s; and my godfather and uncle, John, served aboard USS John F. Kennedy (CV-67) during Vietnam. Finally, my great-uncle, Ray, was a lifelong Merchant Marine. They have had a profound impact on who I am and how I see the world.

Biographies too often read like brag sheets. I will spare you that. The story of my life is simple: extraordinary people have given me wonderful opportunities to live a full life, and my duty now is to say thank you, and to try to be for others what they have been for me.

Richard "Dick" Sherman

John D' Estrada

Charles "Butch" Sherman

Paul "Duke" Garvin

acknowledgements

First, thank you to my wife, Jennifer, for embracing this project and all that went with it. And for joining me on three photo trips including the unforgettable inaugural trip to France in 2018.

A heartfelt thanks to my sister, Joyce, for many things: joining me on a cold trip to Belgium and the Netherlands in November 2018, for editing the book, and for her support along the way.

Thank you to Mary Virginia Swanson who has been a guiding force on this project from the concept stage and then over the bumpy and winding road to its final publication. It is no exaggeration to say that this book would never have been published without her.

My sincere appreciation goes to Vice Admiral Doug Crowder for lending his voice to this project and sharing with us his personal and professional perspective on the importance of our overseas military cemeteries. Thank you, sir.

Thank you to the families of the fallen who shared their stories and photographs. I hope this book reminds everyone of the magnitude of their sacrifice and that of their families and friends.

I'd like to express my gratitude to my marketing assistant, Beth Bagley, for helping in many ways. I appreciate her passionate searches for elusive photos of our fallen heroes and for sharing her infectious joy when she found them.

I would like to thank the individuals at the American Battle Monuments Commission who are dedicated to maintaining a solemn resting place for our war dead. The superintendents and staff were impressive in their knowledge and generous in their support for this project. Lastly, merci bien to Manon Bart in Paris and Ashleigh Byrnes in Arlington, VA.

Thank you to Allen Ashton for his thoughtful and careful design. Allen's enthusiasm for the book added a much-needed spark of energy at exactly the right time.

I am also grateful to Kevin Callahan who has published an excellent book, "Brothers in Arms." It is rare to find someone so generous in sharing their experiences and advice to another author in the same genre. Thanks, Kevin.

Thanks to Joe Mahler, who designed the maps and who was supportive of this project from its earliest days.

Thanks to Alan Kesselhaut for his help with the panoramic image of the World War II veterans at Normandy, and to Dawn Children for proofreading the book and adding her enthusiasm to this project.

And I'd like to thank a mentor, Arthur Meyerson, who once told me to "get messy" in my compositions, and thus opened new avenues of creative expression within the same old frame.

Note: I have used certain words to refer to different races in this book. The terms used are the ones generally accepted to be appropriate and respectful at the time of this writing. I am generally following the 2022 National Archives recommendations for this purpose. Also, I refer to Native Americans who used their languages for communication during the wars as Code Talkers, which is, at present, the commonly used term.

The appropriate terms have changed over time and may change in the future. The book is intended as a journey of gratitude and, thus, the terms are intended to show the greatest respect. There are also quotes in the book, and they may use different words to address race than the ones generally accepted today; I have made no changes to the quotations.

Photo Credits

Photos of Kurt Gruber, Alex Penkala Jr., Charles Summers, James & Robert Tester from Fields of Honor

Photos of George Peters, Ernest Prussman, and Louis Van Schaick from CMOHS website

Photos of Henry Boger courtesy of Ohio State University and With the Colors from Aurora, IL (1917-1919)

Photo of Nelson Bowers courtesy of *The Reading Times*

Photos of the Cromwell Twins from Green-Wood

Photo of George Glenn from *Lynchburg News & Advance*

Photo of Henry Fulghum from the *New York Times*, with special thanks to Lisa Oberg

Photo of George Howe courtesy of US National Library of Medicine

Photo of Teresa Murphy courtesy of the University of New Hampshire

Photos of William Sawelson and his Medal of Honor courtesy of Dr. Steven Sawelson

Photo of Clyde Sherman courtesy of New Albany-Floyd County Public Library, with special thanks to Veronica

Photo of Crosby Whitman courtesy of Harvard University Archives (HUD 367.219.2 Box 2, no. 129)

Photo of John Wickersham courtesy of Don Roche and the American Legion LCW Post One, Denver, CO

Photos of George Zellers courtesy of *Lancaster Journal* and Franklin & Marshall College

Photo of Hazel Bingner courtesy of Bob Jones University and John Matzko

Photos of Robert Cole, Elliott & Sanford Goodman courtesy of Honor States

Photos of Morris and Timothy Counihan courtesy of the Counihan family, with special thanks to Kevin Callahan

Photo of Carlie Dial courtesy of Tim Clark, with special thanks to Kelli Mecifi and the Robeson County Library

Photo of Arthur Dieffenbacher courtesy of Garden City College

Photo of Jonathan Grout from Pomfret High School yearbook

Photo of Roderick Hall from the CIA and Wikimedia

Photo of Raymond Hansen courtesy of Garrett Evangelical Theological Seminary, with special thanks to Daniel Smith, Lynn Berg, and Dr. Lucy Chung

Photo of Leonard Hofstetter from *Peoria News Journal,* with special thanks to Amber Lowry at the Peoria Public Library

Photo of Joseph Hoodock from *The News Journal*

Photo of Mitsulu Miyoko courtesy of *Pacific Citizen*, with special thanks to Susan Yokoyama

Photo of Noboru Miyoko from *Salt Lake Tribune*

Photo of Boyce Nichols from the *Brooklyn Daily Eagle*

Photo of George Patton courtesy of the Virginia Military Institute, with special thanks to Mary Laura Kludy

Photo of Andrew Perry courtesy of the Oklahoma Historical Society, with special thanks to Jon May

Photo of Vernon Preble courtesy of AFS, with special thanks to Andrea Kutsenkow and Jonathan Gross

Photo of Ruben Rivers courtesy of American Legion Post 260 Tecumseh, OK, with special thanks to the Snodgrass family

Photos of Quentin Roosevelt and Wilma Vinsant courtesy of the US Air Force, with special thanks to Dr. Judith Barger

Photos of Maurice Rose courtesy of The Rose Monument, with special thanks to Paul Shamon

Photo of Ward Sackal courtesy of Christine Gorder

Photos of Edmund Searby courtesy of Lucy Melvin (Searby)

Photo of Irving Shure courtesy of *The X-Ray Yearbook*, The Medical College of Virginia (now Virginia Commonwealth University), with special thanks to Mary Kate Brogan and Margaret Truman Kidd

Photo of Alexis Sommaripa courtesy of the Sommaripa family, with special thanks to Nick Sommaripa

Photo of Joe Squirrel courtesy of Diana Cavener

Photo of Glenn Tester courtesy of Frank Tester

If not listed, photos were obtained from various public sources, including but not limited to Wikimedia Commons, the Library of Congress, and the National Archives

Index

Ambrose, Stephen: 90

American Battle Monuments Commission: VII, X, 206, 210, 218, Back Cover

American Battle Monuments Foundation: Back Cover

American Cemeteries

Aisne-Marne American Cemetery, WWI: 13-14, 118-119, 144-145, 166

Ardennes American Cemetery, WWII: 23, 136-137, 152-153, 164-165

Brittany American Cemetery, WWII: 32, 124-125, 146-147

Brookwood American Cemetery, WWI: 21, 98-99, 207, 216-217

Cambridge American Cemetery, WWII: 24-25, 39, 54-55, 64-65, 142-143

Epinal American Cemetery, WWII: 66-67, 84-85, 158-159, 177, 200

Flanders Field American Cemetery, WWI: 22, 27, 60-61, 104-107, 180-181

Florence American Cemetery, WWII: 19, 84-85, 138-139

Henri-Chapelle American Cemetery, WWII: 28-29, 46-47, 78-79, 162, 168, 170-171

Lafayette Escadrille Memorial Cemetery, WWI: 16-17, 201

Lorraine American Cemetery, WWII: 15, 36-37, 114-115, 167, 189

Luxembourg American Cemetery, WWII: 70-73, 90-91, 140-141, 173, 183-184, 186

Manila American Cemetery, WWII: 26, 41, 86-87, 100-101, 120-121, 172, 188

Meuse-Argonne American Cemetery, WWI: 116-117, 126-129, 156, 185, 190, 193-198

Netherlands American Cemetery, WWII: 18, 26, 48-49, 80-81, 94-95, 130-133, 163, 178-179, 187, 191

Normandy American Cemetery, WWII: 5, 30, 33, 35, 42-43, 56-59, 68-69, 82-83, 122-123, 196, 199, 202-205

North Africa American Cemetery, WWII: 20, 74-77, 154-155

Oise-Aisne American Cemetery, WWI: 6-7, 44, 134-135, 145, 192

Rhone American Cemetery, WWII: 50-51, 150-151, 174-176, 182-183

Sicily-Rome American Cemetery, WWII: 39, 40, 88-89, 102-103, 108-109

Somme American Cemetery, WWI: 2-3, 30-31, 38, 52-53, 92-93, 160

St. Mihiel American Cemetery, WWI: XVI, 8-12, 34, 38, 112-113, 148-149, 161, 196, 198

Suresnes American Cemetery, WWI and WWII: 21, 62-63, 96-97, 110-111, 169

American Foreign Service, AFS: 102

Bingner, Hazel: 100-101

Boger, Henry: 148-149

Bowers, Floyd: 145

Bowers, Nelson: 144-145

Bradley, Omar: 69

Brittain, Vera: 157

Chaplain: 54, 57, 58, 134

Charon, Francisco: 142-143

Civilian: 62, 102

Clinton, Bill: 114

Cole, Robert: 132-133

Counihan, Morrison: 88-89

Counihan, Timothy: 88-89

Cromwell, Dorothy: 96-97

Cromwell, Gladys: 96-97

Crowder, Doug: X, XI, 210, Back Cover

Doctor: 61, 62, 65, 94, 133

Dial, Carlie: 152-153

Dieffenbacher, Arthur: 58-59

Draper, Foy: 76-77

Eisenhower, Dwight D.: 70, 133

Fairchild, Helen: 92-93

Friends of the National World War II Memorial: Back Cover

Fulghum, Henry Edgar: 110-111

George, David Lloyd: 4

Glenn, George Preston: 106-107

Goodman, Elliott: 80-81

Goodman, Sanford: 80-81

Grout, Jonathan: 74-75

Gruber, Kurt: 136-137

Hall, Roderick Stephen: 138-139

Hansen, Raymond: 56-57

Harding, Warren: 206

Hofstetter, Leonard: 154-155

Hoodock Jr., Joseph: 74-75

Howe, George: 60-61

Kilmer, Joyce: 134-135

Kocak, Matej: 126-127

Korean War: VIII, X, 208

Lincoln, Abraham: XI

MacArthur, Arthur and Douglas: 69

McMahon, Lynn: Back Cover

Medal of Honor: 68-69, 82-83, 112-133

Merchant Marines: 142, 208

Miyoko, Mitsulu: 84-85

Miyoko, Noboru: 84-85

Monteith, Jimmy: 122-123

Muck, Warren: 90-91

Murphy, Teresa: 98-99

Native American: 146-147, 150-153

Nichols, Boyce: 74-75

Office of Strategic Services, OSS: 136-141

Olympics: 70, 77

Osborne, Weedon: 118-119

Patton, George: 70-71, 114

Pearl Harbor: 85, 86

Penkala Jr., Alex: 90-91

Perry, Andrew: 150-151

Pershing, John: 121, 206

Peters, George: 130-131

Pitts, Oliver "Jack": X

Plato: 1

Preble, Vernon: 102-103

Prussman, Ernest: 124-125

Red Cross: 62-63, 93, 97

Richert, Floyd: 54-55

Rivers, Ruben: 114-115

Roosevelt Jr., Teddy: 57, 68-69, 82-83

Roosevelt, Franklin D.: 45, 206

Roosevelt, Quentin: 82-83

Roosevelt, Theodore: 69, 82

Rose, Maurice: 72-73

Rosener, James: Back Cover

Ross, Mac: 108-109

Royal Air Force, RAF: 49, 105

Sackal, Ward: 50-51

Sawelson, William: 116-117

Searby, Edmund: 66-67

Sherman, Clyde: 52-53

Shure, Irving: 64-65

Sommaripa, Alexis: 140-141

Squirrel, Joe Little: 146-147

Stowers, Freddie: 128-129

Sullivan, Albert: 86-87

Sullivan, Francis: 86-87

Sullivan, George: 86-87

Sullivan, Joseph: 86-87

Sullivan, Madison: 86-87

Summers, Charles: 48-49

Tester, Glenn: 78-79

Tester, James: 78-79

Tester, Robert: 78-79

Tuskegee: 109, 149

US Air Force, USAF: 206, 208

US Army Air Force, USAAF: 49, 50, 54, 77, 94, 109, 125, 153

US Army Nurse Corps: 93, 98

US Army, USA: 52, 57, 58, 61, 65, 66, 69, 70, 73, 78, 81, 82, 85, 89, 90, 101, 102, 105, 106, 110, 113, 114, 117, 121, 122, 125, 129, 130, 133, 134, 141, 145, 146, 149, 150, 154, 206

US Coast Guard, USCG: 74, 217

US Marine Corps, USMC: VIII, 118, 126, 206, 208

US Navy, USN: VI, VIII-IX, 69, 86, 118, 125, 208, Back Cover

USS Tampa: 217

van Schaick, Louis: 120-121

Vietnam: VIII, XV, 208

Vinsant, Wilma: 94-95

Whitman, Crosby Church: 62-63

Wickersham, John Hunter: 112-113

Zellers, George: 104-105

BROOKWOOD

LES WESLEY J	BOY 1C	USCGC TAMPA	SEPT 26 1918	FLO
RWOOD ROBERT	BOY 1C	USCGC TAMPA	SEPT 26 1918	FLO
ESEN MARTIN M	FIREMAN	USCGC SENECA	SEPT 17 1918	DENM
RKIN CHARLES W	BOY 1C	USCGC TAMPA	SEPT 26 1918	RHODE IS
PPELL FELIX G	SEAMAN	USCGC TAMPA	SEPT 26 1918	FLO
ULSEN ANDERS	ASST MSTR AT ARMS	USCGC TAMPA	SEPT 26 1918	DENM
ME WILLIAM HEERMANCE	SEAMAN GUNNER	USCGC SENECA	SEPT 17 1918	NEW
IGLEY FRANK H	ACTG CARPENTER 2C	USCGC TAMPA	SEPT 26 1918	CONNECT
YNOLDS WILLIAM H	SEAMAN	USCGC TAMPA	SEPT 26 1918	GEO
HARDS JOHN I	SEAMAN	USCGC TAMPA	SEPT 26 1918	MASSACHUS
BERTS PERRY	COOK	USCGC TAMPA	SEPT 26 1918	MARYL
BERTSON ROBERT G	BOY 1C	USCGC TAMPA	SEPT 26 1918	ALA
SS JIMMIE	BOY 1C	USCGC TAMPA	SEPT 26 1918	FLO
DARINI ALEXANDER L	ACTG QMSTR	USCGC TAMPA	SEPT 26 1918	NEW JE
RKIN MICHAEL	SEAMAN	USCGC TAMPA	SEPT 26 1918	MASSACHUS
TERLEE CHARLES	CAPTAIN	USCGC TAMPA	SEPT 26 1918	CONNECT
LLY ARCHIBALD HOWARD	CAPTAIN	USCGC TAMPA	SEPT 26 1918	MARYL
WEGLER PAUL B	SEAMAN	USCGC TAMPA	SEPT 26 1918	MISS
TT FRANCIS R	FIREMAN	USCGC TAMPA	SEPT 26 1918	MICH
ANAHAN EDWARD F	ACTG BAYMAN	USCGC TAMPA	SEPT 26 1918	NEW JE
CKLEN IRVING A	BOY 1C	USCGC TAMPA	SEPT 26 1918	NEW Y
TH JOHN	COXSWAIN	USCGC TAMPA	SEPT 26 1918	
LLENWERF MERTON	SEAMAN	USCGC SENECA	SEPT 17 1918	NEW Y
NER HOMER B	SEAMAN	USCGC TAMPA	SEPT 26 1918	

AMERICAN BATTLE MONUMENTS COMMISSION
UNITED STATES
OF AMERICA